From Wilderness to Worship

A 40 Day Journey

by
JT SEDORY

JT [signature]

Printed in the United States of America

First Printing, 2019

ISBN-13: 978-1791680404
ISBN-10: 1791680402

Scripture quotes included in this publication are from the following versions:

Unless otherwise noted, all Scripture is taken from the New King James Version. Copyright © 1982 by Thomas Nelson, Inc. Used by permission. All rights reserved.

Quotations designated (NIV) are from THE HOLY BIBLE, NEW INTERNATIONAL VERSION® NIV®
Copyright © 1973, 1978, 1984, 2011 by International Bible Society®
Used by permission. All rights reserved worldwide.

Scripture quotations marked NLT are taken from the *Holy Bible,* New Living Translation, copyright © 1996, 2004, 2007. Used by permission of Tyndale House Publishers, Inc.,
Carol Stream, Illinois 60188. All rights reserved.

Scripture quotations marked NASB are taken from the NEW AMERICAN STANDARD BIBLE, © Copyright The Lockman Foundation 1960, 1962, 1963, 1968, 1971, 1972, 1973, 1975, 1977, 1988, 1995. Used by permission.

I dedicate this book to my Lord and Savior, Jesus Christ.
Also, to my wife Terri, along with our grown children,
Kevin, Justin, Lauren and Megan.
Without them, this book would never have been possible.

TABLE OF CONTENTS

Preface

A.W. Tozer wrote, *"The only book that should ever be written is the one that flows up from the heart, forced out by the inward pressure... The man who is thus charged with a message will not be turned back by any blasé consideration. His book will be to him not only imperative, it will be inevitable."* [1]

This book has been a passion of mine to share, that has become a reality, *only*—and I must emphasize *only*—by the grace of God and the leading of the Holy Spirit. I believe it was burning in my heart for years, and it took precise events in my life orchestrated by God—some of which you'll read about—to bring it to fruition.

Not long ago, the Lord brought back to my memory, some things that occurred to me as a young teenager. In fact, it wasn't until this book was half-written that I recalled what had happened years prior. They had impacted me more than I had realized.

One of those events was when I was home alone, sitting in my living room, listening to some Christian music. Suddenly, I felt an overwhelming sense of the presence of God and His conviction of my sin. I remember crying and asking for Him to forgive me. I believe now, that it was at that moment in my life I was saved and that I trusted Jesus Christ as my Savior. Because He called me, I must give Him glory and praise.

The second memory that came back, not long after the first, was when I was *preaching* from a make-shift podium in my bedroom. My captive audience at the time was my Aunt Dorothy and her boyfriend. Even at that early age, I knew I had a desire to preach. I even pictured standing before a large audience proclaiming God's word, something I've been privileged to do often.

---

[1] A.W. Tozer, *God's Pursuit of Man* (©1950, renewed 1978 by Lowell Tozer), Preface. Emphasis mine.

Those events took place in 1974. What significance does that have in my life? Fast forward to 2014.

I was on my way home from Houston, TX, where some friends of mine, Jerry and Donna Williams[2] live. I'd spent a few days with them in their home, on what I know now, was a divinely ordained visit. While I was there, I asked for details on an internship program they offered to be ordained through EPIC Ministries. On my motorcycle ride home, God spoke to my heart that preaching His word was the *call* on my life. It was finally time to go into the Promised Land. From the wilderness, to worship, after wandering in the desert for 40 years—1974 to 2014.

---

[2] "Jerry Williams," epicministries.org/about/jerry/ (accessed December 7, 2018).

Dedication

Trust in the Lord with all your heart and lean not
on your own understanding; In all your ways
acknowledge Him, and He shall direct your paths.
Proverbs 3:5-6

This book is dedicated to my father, John Daniel Sedory. He was born on March 29, 1923 and went to his heavenly home, to be with the Lord he loved and served most of his life, on March 29, 2013. Yes, it was on his 90th birthday.

My father was never wealthy according to the world's standards of riches, but the inheritance he left us with was one of the greatest treasures he ever could have; it was a book about his life.

One of the chapters in this book you are reading is about my parents. In it I'll share a few more things about them and how God specifically answered my prayers for them both.

I miss them both very much. There are so many things I wish I could have talked to them about since they've been gone. It's hard to believe that as I write this, it's already been just over four years since they left us.

Proverbs 3:5-6 was Dad's life verse, and I think he believed it and lived it out daily when he didn't understand the way things worked out for him at times. He accepted things as God made His path for him, even in the most difficult days.

"Dad, I love you more than words can describe, and I thank you for being such a great father, one who encouraged me, prayed for me, and was a living example of what a husband and father should be. I dedicate this book to you. Until the day I meet Jesus and see you again, I love you very much."

Introduction

Everybody has a story. I have one, and you have one. Whether you think you do or not, I'm telling you right now, your story is unique and unlike any other. To you, life may seem plain, ordinary, and mundane. But, even in those moments, when you don't think you've made a lick of difference in your life or in anyone else's life, I promise, you have.

I won't get into the whole DNA thing, which I'm still amazed at (as are many scientists who discover things all the time), but I do know there is no other DNA exactly like yours among 7.3 billion people on planet Earth. That makes you unique in the sight of your Creator.

This forty-day journey you are about to read is just a glimpse at my story. However, my story didn't take forty days; it took forty years. As you read these short devotionals, I hope to share with you some things about me and what I have learned about walking in the wilderness; to finally arriving at worship.

Most of these devotionals are taken from real-life events and the amazing things from my journey through life with God who never once left me. There are Scripture verses to start with each day, most of them are from the New King James Version. It is my hope God will use them to draw you closer to Him. My entire life is founded on the very word of God and my personal relationship with Him is essential as His Word feeds me daily.

My wilderness story is like the children of Israel in many ways. When I felt the call on my life to go and possess what I had been given (eternal life; my promised land) rather than obey the call from God, I wandered far too many years.

A.C.T.S.

When Saul saw the Philistine army, he was afraid; terror filled his heart. He inquired of the LORD, but the LORD did not answer him by dreams or Urim or prophets. Saul then said to his attendants, "Find me a woman who is a medium, so I may go and inquire of her."
1 Samuel 28:5-7 (NIV)

For those of you that can remember and even lived during the seventies and eighties, you'll remember the video game craze that took place back then. Everywhere you went there were arcades and games where you could take your spare change or even your hard-earned money, if you were truly addicted to the flashing screens and challenge of getting to the next level and drop it in the slots for another chance to be recognized for the top score of the day!

There were some places however, where you couldn't use your money (US coins). You had to exchange it for tokens that worked in *their* machines. A lot of those coins had their names and logos on them, along with catchy words and attractive imagery of their business. They gladly and conveniently provided these machines and placed them in easily accessible locations.

Some of these change machines even attracted customers by giving five tokens for the price of $1.00! What a deal, right? But who could stop with only $1.00? You had to get at least a few or more so that if your game stopped and time was running out, you could easily drop in another token and keep right on playing to the next level.

Oh, the memories I have as I even think about the games I used to play myself. I was fortunate enough during those video game days, I used to work in a pizza and sandwich business that had several games. The cool part about working there? I had keys to the games and could play as often and as much as time allowed...FOR FREE (but only when it was slow, or I was on my break, of course)! All I had to do was open the door, find the backside of where the coins normally dropped down, and click away with as many plays as I wanted. It was heaven on earth to any addicted gamer at the time.

One of the many things that happened over an extended period for any of the 'players' back then is that a lot of people would end up with several of these tokens from stores where they had played. You know, a couple of extra ones they dropped in their pockets and emptied at the end of the day. They started to accumulate over time and seldom did the people intentionally grab them and go back, but they would just get more as they went.

If never used again, these tokens were basically useless, good for nothing coins.

So, what do these tokens have to do with the title of this chapter? Specifically, I'd like to draw you to the subject of prayer.

Saul was anointed as King by Samuel the prophet. He was the King. In the beginning, he was worth something, and he followed God. I wonder what his prayers were like when he first became King. No doubt, from where he came from, he must have been quite humbled at becoming a great King of a nation. But, slowly his heart changed, and pride became his god. We see a serious mistake (sin) take place when, after Samuel had died, Saul consulted a medium because he was terrified of the Philistine army.

But what really changed in Saul's heart? I'll go out on a limb here and say that he went from complete dependency on God to depending on himself. His prayers changed too, that I can guarantee you. His adoration of God became twisted to where the only time he prayed is when he was in trouble.

What about you? Ask yourself the following questions. How long do I pray? How often do I pray? Where do I pray? What are my prayers about? Do they mainly contain requests for myself? For others? Could they even be summed up as "bless me thank you" prayers? Trust me; I've fallen prey to this way of praying often. It's easy to fall back into if you don't keep a deep love and devotion to the Lord.

Here's something I have learned and have often practiced over the years. Let's look at look at each of the letters in the acronym A.C.T.S.:

'A' stands for Adoration.
'C' stands for Confession.
'T' stands for Thanksgiving.
'S' stands for Supplication.

I gave you the whole story about the tokens to illustrate your prayer life. Are we just offering God our 'token' prayers that are worthless? At one time, they may have held value, but over time, repetition of the same words (reciting by rote) made them token prayers. Only you would know the answer to that question.

I'd like to suggest something that will help you. First, if you feel a desire to change your prayer life, don't read more books on the subject. Don't join discussions on how others pray or go to seminars that will teach you how better to pray. My suggestion is simple. Pray. That's right, pray. If you can hold a one sentence conversation with someone, you can pray. I'm certain you can speak more than one sentence at a time.

If you're still hitting a wall when you pray, follow the acronym I gave you. 'A' for adoration simply means you begin by talking to God about Himself. He is all-powerful and all-knowing. He is love, full of grace, mercy, forgiveness, healing, and a thousand more attributes. What you're doing is *adoring God* for who He is when you speak these things back to Him. It opens the opportunity for you to begin worshipping Him for Who He is!

Next is the letter 'C' for confession. There's nothing a loving Father would love to hear more than His child coming to him to restore a broken relationship. It is keeping your slate clean. Why do we do this after worship? Because it draws us into a closer union with Him when we are forgiven. He takes us into His presence and we feel clean.

'T' is the next letter, which stands for thanksgiving. Oh, the depth of praise we could give Him at this point in our prayers for ALL He has done! His forgiveness, His provision, His blessings; the very breath we have, the beat of our hearts, the things we can do with our senses; ALL things we can thank Him for. Read the Psalms to find ways to give Him thanksgiving.

'S' stands for 'supplication,' which simply means requests. There is nothing wrong with asking God for things. However, we tend to linger on this subject a lot longer than we should. What we think we need, and what we really need are quite often two different things. I think the best thing we can do when requesting, or asking Him something, is to ask for the needs of others. There are a multitude of people in this world much worse off than we are. Plus, when our focus is on praying for others, it makes light of our seemingly hard issues and fulfills one of the greatest commandments to *"love your neighbor as yourself."*

One of the greatest resources that has helped in my prayer life was a booklet written by K.P. Yohannan, founder of Gospel for Asia. It's called, *Learning to Pray*. In it, Yohannan mentions several things about what prayer is, what it isn't, and how prayer is misunderstood. I highly recommend you get a copy for yourself. One of the many points he makes in the book that made an impact on me was this: *"We could read every book ever written on prayer, but that won't make us people of prayer. We learn to pray by doing it."*[3] Also, *"The most important thing is that you pray!* As you pray, the Lord will show you more of His heart in prayer and what He desires from you."[4]

I will close by asking you a question, or really a personal assessment of your prayer life. Do you treat your prayer life as "token prayers" when your options have run out or what you want isn't happening? Or, do you pray as with a genuine, heartfelt, intimacy, with God?

---

[3] *Learning to Pray* (©2004 by K.P. Yohannan), p. 14. Emphasis mine.
[4] Ibid., p. 55. [See: gfa.org/resource/books/learning-to-pray/; accessed 12/19/2018.]

A Near Miss

*Praying always with all prayer and supplication in the Spirit, being **watchful** to this end with all perseverance and supplication for all the saints.   (Ephesians 6:18; emphasis mine)*

My family and I have lived in Memphis Tennessee now for over twenty years. We moved from California where we would rarely encounter deer running across the road. There were more possibilities in certain areas of the state, so during our visits to such places we'd always joke about the yellow signs along the side of the road that say "jumping deer" ahead.

Sightings here (and close encounters of the deer kind) are a much more common occurrence. Depending on the season, some of those encounters can be quite hazardous or even deadly.

Such was the case with my near miss that took place one evening as I drove home from work. It was nearing dusk, and I was driving about 65 miles per hour, the speed limit for that section of the highway. My eyes are used to scanning the horizon, especially with the contrast of the darker ground against the glowing orange sunset. This kind of constant eye movement and scanning as I drive is a practice I learned early on, used especially when riding my motorcycle. The highway is mostly straight, and it would be very easy to lose concentration during my commute to and from work.

On this night, out of nowhere, a 4-point buck (yes, he was close enough that I could count the tines) came from the median on my left side, and it looked as if I would hit him head-on with my car. Had it not been for the actions I took, hitting the brakes and, laying on the horn, which initially scared him enough that he turned momentarily, I would have surely hit him, and by his size, he would have come crashing through my windshield causing severe damage, or even worse, my demise.

I'm sure a lot of you reading this have had similar situations happen to you or loved ones, but this event got me thinking about something spiritually that takes place in the life of every Christian as well.

Grab your bible and read 1 Peter 5:8. If you're like me, you may want to underline this verse and even commit it to memory. It says, "Stay alert! Watch out for your great enemy, the devil. He prowls around like a roaring lion, looking for someone to devour" (NLT).

Strolling idly along in this Christian life is not an option. It's as if we're engaged in war and we need to have our weapons always drawn (see 2 Corinthians 10:4). Had I been playing around with the radio, talking on my phone, or worse, taking my eyes off the road for longer than I should, that evening's drive home would have turned out quite differently.

So, what are we supposed to be doing to prevent the possibility of being *devoured* by our enemy? If there's one thing the enemy hates more than God, it is His Word! "For the word of God *is* living and powerful, and sharper than any two-edged sword, piercing even to the division of soul and spirit, and of joints and marrow, and is a discerner of the thoughts and intents of the heart" (Hebrews 4:12).

What did Jesus do in the desert when being tempted by Satan? He used the Word to fight off the attack of the enemy. Not reason, not argument, not compromising, He stood firm on the Word of God.

We should crave God's word and 'digest' it as much as we crave actual food. Whenever I hear about Christians that rarely read God's word or pray, I wonder how they can survive spiritually. Would they go a week or longer without eating just because they're "too busy?"

Preparation is the fundamental key to avoiding dangers, be it a deer crossing the road, a trial or temptation, the loss of a loved one, standing strong in the storms of life or whatever may come your way. That's why the military and first responders train so heavily and emphasize being ready.

When going into battle, any warrior, any Christian, must have a made-up mind. Preparation is needed to use all the pieces of God's armor (see Ephesians 6:10-18). The training, the instruction, the equipping, all come because of time spent in prayer, as it says at the end of the description of the armor: "praying always with all prayer and supplication in the Spirit, being watchful to this end with all perseverance and supplication for all the saints--" (v. 18).

The *real* battle is the one we believers face on our knees and on our faces before God. Satan could care less if we go to church, listen to sermons, go to bible studies, or even witness! What he cares about more than anything, what he fears the most, what he hates, is what is accomplished in prayer, for it is the preparation for the battle in which he'll be defeated!

Some other verses I'd like to draw your attention to deal with being watchful. The first is: "praying always with all prayer and supplication in the Spirit, being **watchful** to this end with all perseverance and supplication for all the saints" (Eph. 6:18; emphasis mine). The implication in that verse is to be always watchful, always praying, always alert. Another great verse is Matthew 26:41: "Watch and pray so that you will not fall into temptation. The spirit is willing, but the flesh is weak" (NIV). As he was about to go further into the Garden of Gethsemane, Jesus told His disciples to watch and pray, because He knew what was about to happen. Only when praying 'in the Spirit' can we overcome the flesh.

Please don't think you can put your Christian cruise-control on in this life and just sit back and relax and take it easy. You never know what may cross your path and catch you off-guard. Remember, be watchful....and PRAY!

A River

My brethren, count it all joy when you fall into various trials, knowing that the testing of your faith produces patience. But let patience have its perfect work, that you may be perfect and complete, lacking nothing.
James 1:2-4

I was departing Memphis International Airport bound for California with a layover in Dallas, Texas. Looking out my window, I enjoyed a majestic view of the "Mighty Mississippi". As I stared at that great river flowing through the land below, I was amazed at how many twists and turns comprise its makeup. A river with such strength and massive currents took a turn every time it was faced with an obstacle.

The river reminded me of myself more than I care to admit. Perhaps you know what I mean by taking the *easier* way out. You've most likely heard it described as *the path of least resistance.*

What do you do when you have a list of things to do, be it a mental or written list? Do you start with the easier things or the harder things? I remember years ago, John MacArthur, Pastor of Grace Community Church in Van Nuys, California, shared something that he believed helped him through school and seminary. He always took on the most difficult, most challenging task first. Then things became easier as he worked his way through his assignments.

Do you think it possible that sometimes struggles, twists and turns, and even a complete direction change is what God uses to strengthen us?

Look, for example, at an egg. Sitting in an incubator for hours, one might observe after a while how it begins to move. Then, a crack in the shell. Before you know it, you can see a tiny beak struggling to break away more of that shell. If you didn't know better, you might even say its struggle seemed as if it was trapped and suffocating. Poor little baby chick, maybe somebody should help the little guy by cracking some of the shell away for him so it's easier for him to get out. But, guess what? People have done that before and as soon as the little chick was completely out, by someone's help, it lay still and died.

What that little chick needed to do, was to go through the struggle of cracking that shell away, slowly, taking its time, building its strength and its ability to stay alive.

Sometimes that's what we need, too—a struggle, a resistance, a challenge, a trial, a literal wall. Take heart, my friend. It is God Himself allowing something to happen to slow us down. Had He not, we might never have known His strength being built up in us for a future situation. Look at how the writer of Hebrews puts it: "For the time being no discipline brings joy, but seems sad *and* painful; yet to those who have been trained by it, afterwards it yields the peaceful fruit of righteousness [right standing with God and a lifestyle and attitude that seeks conformity to God's will and purpose]"[5] (Hebrews 12:11; AMP).

After my Mississippi River observation, it occurred to me that sometimes Christians are like that river. We are *flowing* through this life, but are we, like that river, taking *the path of least resistance?* Are we afraid to share our faith when the opportunity arises? Do we let tough times slow us down and then suddenly change direction and turn away from God? And rather than face our trials, do we turn this way and that way? We may not do it intentionally, but in small areas of our lives do we depend less and less on Him and more and more on ourselves?

Before you know it, we're all *bent* out of shape like a twisted river. Yes, we will have trials; yes, we will face challenging times; and yes, we may even be dragged over the coals for our faith. But, that's the good news. Yes, good news. It is God's promise to us that when we face opposition for His sake, we are to *count it all joy* (see James 1:2). When we come to Jesus and accept His free gift of eternal life, we accept it with His promises. He promised opposition from the world. He promised that we would be despised at times. He promised ridicule and, in some countries, even death for our beliefs. Sharing our faith isn't always easy. At times, we don't want to step out of our comfort zone. But remember, "...He who is in you is greater than he who is in the world" (see 1 John 4:4).

He can and will make the crooked bends in your life a thing of beauty, if you will allow Him to live and work through you.

I can hear you say, "JT, you just don't understand what's happening in my life right now. You've never walked in my shoes. You've never been through the tragedies I have. You have no right to simply say that God will make the crooked bends in my life beautiful."

You may not have put it in those exact words, but if you feel I'm making light of letting God live and work through you, let me ask you a question. If, and I'm assuming for a minute that you at least acknowledge the existence of God, if He is God, and He created the world by the very words He spoke, and created man out of dust and a woman from a rib, is there anything you think God can't do? Only you can answer that.

This isn't a debate on the creation or the existence of God. However, when I've talked with people who are faced with seemingly impossible walls in their lives, it seems to me they're the ones trying to fix it or get the opinion of ten other friends to see what they think, so they can act on the popular vote. Here's a tough question for you. Have you prayed about whatever your struggle is more than you've talked about it?

The God of creation, the God who sent His Only Son to pay the price for our sin on Calvary, is ready, willing, and able to bear your burden. Give it to Him, won't you?

Please take the time to look up the following Scriptures and let each one take you from your struggles into His rest.

1 Peter 5:6-7, Psalm 55:22, Matthew 11:28-30, Hebrews 11 and 12

Are You Clean?

Now thanks *be* to God who always leads us in triumph in Christ,
and through us diffuses the fragrance of His knowledge in every
place. For we are to God the fragrance of Christ among those
who are being saved and among those who are perishing.
2 Corinthians 2:14-15

One of the things I enjoyed about moving from California to
Tennessee was how many more places there were to go fishing. Fishing
must have been in my blood, because my parents and even grandparents
on my Dad's side loved to fish. Although I don't have a lot of memories of
fishing when I was younger, just from the pictures I've seen, it looked like
we all had fun, and often.

I used to take my kids fishing while they were growing up in
California, and again after we moved here. Seems to me I was passing on
to the next generation what I'd learned from the ones that passed it on
to me. There were always fond memories surrounding those times with
the kids. Perhaps they will keep up the tradition.

One of the many things I observed about fishing, was that the
weather, the time of day, the bait you would use, the test of the line—
they would all make a difference. There is a magnitude of details I could
go into about fishing, and even as you read this, you may have had some
of your own memories come to mind.

What I'd like to focus on is just one aspect of fishing—the water.
Without an exhaustive list on those conditions, let's narrow the
conditions down to a lake or a pond. One thing is for certain, and forgive
the obvious conclusion here; you're only going to catch fish, where fish
live.

You're thinking to yourself, "Boy, is this guy a few cards shy of a
full deck, or what?" Bear with me. The fish can only live where the water
conditions are right. And what keeps the conditions right, so they'll live?

A lake or pond where water comes in and water goes out. A constant renewing of the water.

One of my favorite fishing spots is at a friend's house. There are a couple spots where you will see green slime floating at the top and it would appear there were no fish below the surface. But with the right bait, you could land a very nice sized large-mouth bass. The reason they are there is because the water in the rest of the lake is alive, having an inlet and an outlet.

If you were to try and fish at a lake where there was no incoming source of water and no outgoing source of water, mind you, there can't be just one of those (I'll explain that part in a moment), you would not find anything worth catching in there except some mosquitoes and other various bugs.

In case you haven't seen where this is going yet, allow me to start drawing a vivid picture for you.

All Christians need to be fed the word of God and all Christians need to give out the word of God. Using the exact illustration, I gave about a healthy source of water coming in and going out, what would a Christian be with only one or the other? Or for that matter, neither one?

Let's look at the inlet only source for a Christian.

Without leaving you to wonder what I mean by a Christian, allow me to define what I believe a Christian is: one who has become a Christ follower, who has believed on the Lord Jesus Christ and has confessed with his mouth, turned (repented) from his wicked ways (sins), and now trusts Him to be Lord of his life. That is the biblical definition of a Christian.

We have a Christ follower (as defined above). He begins his walk with the Lord. He goes to church each time the doors are open. He reads his bible and prays daily. He listens to Christian radio. He even starts to memorize Scripture. That sounds like a Christian full of life, right? What if that's all he did? Nothing more. No fellowship. No witnessing. No sharing what happened to him with others. It will only be a matter of time where that person becomes stagnant, like the lake or the pond that starts to stink.

You're certainly able to disagree with my statement but let me illustrate that for you. Where would the church be today if a certain man who got radically saved on a certain road a long time ago, never shared what Jesus did for him? I'll tell you where we would be. We would have no idea who Paul was, we would have 13 letters missing from the bible, and we would have much of God's word missing in our lives (not that God couldn't have done it without him, but He did use him).

Now let's take the outlet only source for a Christian.

It's impossible really if you think about it. For one to be saved, there would have to have been something (in this case, Jesus) that would have come in prior to one being able to be saved in the first place. For the sake of illustration, let's say that happened. Then, nothing. Unlike the person we first mentioned, this Christian started sharing what happened. Sounds good, right? He's witnessing. That's good, right?

One problem, he is not fellowshipping with other believers at church or anywhere else for that matter. He is not ready, memorizing the word, and he is not even praying. He is counting on that one-time "I got saved back on such-and-such date" to carry him through the rest of his life. But he keeps trying on his own, of course, to pour out what little he has into others. Guess what? Before long, he is empty, dried up, lifeless. Like water in a lake or pond that is being drained with nothing new coming in, eventually the water will run out. There's no place for life left.

Finally, let's look at a healthy Christian.

A believer and follower of Jesus Christ who is continually feeding on the word of God, along with all other sources of fresh, biblical, sound doctrine, time alone with the Savior, sitting daily at His feet, allowing the Holy Spirit to lead him daily—a person like that cannot help but feed others the way he has been fed. His heart's desire is to share the simple message of the gospel—the good news—with others. It is his very passion in life. A Christian like that has abundant life!

So, I close by asking you to consider where you are my friend. Which type of lake or pond are you? Are you a source of living water as we looked at above? Or are you a stagnant Christian with nothing coming in and nothing going out. Or worse, only one or the other? Are you a body of fresh water, or do you stink?

You do not have to remain unchanged if you feel the Holy Spirit tugging at your heart to change where you are. Be honest with God; He can take it. Ask Him to teach you and show you how to be that source of fresh water today!

Are You Hungry?

But He answered and said, "It is written, 'Man shall not live by bread alone, but by every word that proceeds from the mouth of God.'"
Matthew 4:4

Simply stated, Jesus Christ has radically changed my life. If He didn't, I would never have written this 40-day devotional. But, because He has, I am passionate about His love for me and I hunger for His word daily! That is what motivates me to share these devotionals with you. What I'm about to share with you could change your destiny in life. I pray it does.

Obviously, everybody gets hungry. We are designed to eat food to sustain life. We hunger, and then we eat, otherwise we'd starve to death. Food and water are essential for any life, and without it, there is no life. We were designed that way. God knew what He was doing when He created us. Funny thing is—or at least in my experience—I can stuff myself at a buffet, and an hour later, I'm feeling hungry again!

God also designed us to have a hunger and thirst for Him. But the void is filled in many other ways. Some with too much activity, as if they thrive on being busy from sun up till sun down. Others with recreation, entertainment, socializing, sports, and so on. They spare no time for what's most important. All that *busyness* offers temporary satisfaction, and then after the excitement is over, they can still feel *empty* inside just like then buffet with food.

I firmly believe that a lot of people feel empty because they don't believe they have a purpose in life. They attempt to *fill* themselves and find satisfaction in many ways. They try it with sex, drugs, alcohol, violence, success, money, entertainment, and anything else they can. You may be one of those people searching to be filled. You may be trying to fill that void right now. God designed you with a desire to be filled with something, but not just food or the other things I mentioned.

God designed you to have a relationship with Him, and to desire Him. To be completely satisfied with Him. To have nothing else above him. In Matthew 4:4, the Bible says, "But He answered and said, "It is written, man shall not live by bread alone, but by every word that proceeds from the mouth of God.'"'

It's more than just food and water we need to be filled and complete; it is the Word of God that we need to sustain us and to have real life. Jesus is the Bread from Heaven, broken for us on the cross, so that we feed on His words, and on Him living in us and through us.

It's hard for me to describe what it feels like when I know the Lord Jesus is working in and through me. His word is *alive and powerful* (see Hebrews 4:12). Jesus is the Bread of Life, and the Living Water. Jesus said, "I am the bread of life. He who comes to Me will never hunger, and he who believes in Me will never thirst" (John 6:35).

Do you long to be satisfied? Do you need purpose? Do you hunger for something but just can't quite figure out what that is? You can have that emptiness filled when you come to the only One that can fill it. Even if you know you're saved, you can feel lost in the wilderness.

Jesus said in Matthew 5:6, "Blessed *are* those who hunger and thirst for righteousness, for they will be filled."

Many years ago, I was trying to find that satisfaction to life, to fill that void I felt inside. I did it with alcohol. I could not go a day without it. It didn't matter what time of day it was, I thought I needed to drink to be satisfied, to be happy. I was trying to fill the emptiness and void in my life. But what it did was almost ruin my marriage.

Only by God's grace and His word was it possible my wife and I could survive in our nearly broken marriage—the one I attempted to shipwreck.

If you are searching right now for satisfaction in anything other than God Himself, I'm here to offer you a better solution. From one beggar to another, from one who discovered the Living Bread of life, your search can be over once and for all. Fill yourself on the bread that will give you genuine satisfaction!

Are You Overwhelmed?

Hear my cry, O God; Attend to my prayer. From the end of the earth
I will cry to You, When my heart is overwhelmed; Lead me to the rock
that is higher than I. For You have been a shelter for me,
A strong tower from the enemy. I will abide in Your tabernacle
forever; I will trust in the shelter of Your wings.
Psalm 61:1-4

Have you ever felt like there were about 10 (or more) things pulling you in different directions all at the same time? It's almost as if you need a 30-hour day to get it all done. Have you ever been there? Are you there right now?

One of the ways people describe being overwhelmed, is to say they're *busy.* When I feel overwhelmed, or *busy,* I've jokingly told people, "I feel like my noodles are sliding off my plate."

Instead of spending time making a detailed list of all the things on your mind right now (which I doubt will help you clear your mind at all), you may find it easier to begin by putting all those things in categories— in other words, in the order of importance or priority. But before you even start with that, keep reading a little more.

Has anyone ever told you that you were OCD? Better yet, let's spell out what that means: *Obsessive Compulsive Disorder.* I'll go out on a limb and say that if you're a person easily overwhelmed, it's because you're OCD. On more than one occasion I've been told that. I looked it up and found it encompasses a few different behavioral traits. Look and see if you fall into one of these forms as well:

"Ordering (having things in order) is a subcategory [of OCD] (behavior) where persons feel compelled to place items in a designated spot or order. This person fears a sense of being overwhelmed and impending anarchy if items are not placed exactly as they are arbitrarily determined. Persons with this condition typically line up items in parallel locations, but the focus is on the concept that each item belongs in a specific place. Another form of OCD is **perfectionism**, in which persons feel compelled to habitually check for potential mistakes or errors that might reveal their own faults or might jeopardize the person's stature at work."[6]

The crazy thing in the definition above is that I know I will NEVER accomplish complete perfectionism in my life and that trying to do it all perfect makes me feel overwhelmed.

I'll tell you what else happens when you are OCD and make a feeble attempt at perfectionism. The very things you struggle with, are the very things you tend to be the pickiest about in other people's lives. It can also flow out in an attitude toward others and damage relationships.

The irony in all this though is how we can expect others to be a certain way when we can't even help ourselves in those same certain areas.

Romans 2:1 helps me see my problem clearly. It says: "You may think you can condemn such people [point out their faults], but you are just as bad, and you have no excuse! When you say, they are wicked [or don't do the things you do, or the way you do them] and should be punished, you are condemning yourself, for you who judge others do these very same things" (NLT; comments in brackets are mine).

This could easily lead us into the subject of forgiveness, but since this is about being overwhelmed, I'll let the forgiveness topic speak for itself in later chapters.

What else happens to you when you are feeling overwhelmed? Don't you start to focus on yourself more? Don't your problems, your busyness, your life seem to matter the most then? You start to have a party, and you're the only one invited.

---

[6] "What is O.C.D.?", by Steven Phillipson, Ph.D., prisontalk.com/forums/showthread.php?t=217210 (comments in parentheses and emphasis are mine); also see: ocdonline.com/whatisocd .

It might not be a bad idea to start thinking about writing that category list now. But do it with others in mind. Perplexed on that suggestion? What I mean is this: since such a list should be based on priorities, what is supposed to be number one in your life? Let me rephrase that. *Who* is supposed to be your number one priority? God. If not, why not? Again, that's a subject for another chapter.

There's one last thought I have on being overwhelmed, and let's not park on that word but rather look for a way to start our engines and get moving right along. It's what you really need the most when you feel overwhelmed. Care to guess? May I suggest that it's comfort? I'm not talking about an arm around you from a friend during your pity party saying, *"Poor baby, you just need a big ol' hug right now. Dry your tears, it's going to be okay."*

No, what you really need is comfort! And there's only One that can provide you with that overwhelming sense of comfort. He provides it to those in need, does he not? Try a word study on the word comfort and see how God supplies it for those in need. David, Job, Isaiah, and many others were comforted by God in their times of need. After reading about their lives, do you think they were overwhelmed a time or two?

So, I conclude with one of the greatest verses I know about comfort. It's found in
2 Corinthians 1:3-4: "Blessed *be* the God and Father of our Lord Jesus Christ, the Father of mercies and God of all comfort, who comforts us in all our tribulation, that we may be able to comfort those who are in any trouble, with the comfort with which we ourselves are comforted by God."

Are You Prepared to Die?

And just as each person is destined to
die once and after that comes judgment.
Hebrews 9:27 (NLT)

Please don't take what you're about to read as criticism. I may get some grimaced faces (which I'll never see) or some emails (which I *will* read), but give me a little grace, okay?

Are you ready? I'm not much into country music (okay, you read it, now let's move on and hopefully you'll see I'm not that mean). That's right, I just don't like it; never have, probably never will. Now that may not be too popular among the Southerner's, but I mean no offense by it. The reason I state that is because until my youngest daughter Megan brought a song to my attention many years ago, which I'd not heard before, although at the time it was apparently very popular, I thought it was all nonsense.

She had bought the CD (remember those things?) and played this one song repeatedly. I was very impressed with the lyrics of this song. Plus, since first hearing this song, I even went to a concert with Megan and heard the artist sing in person. I was suddenly hooked on that one song (no, I didn't say hooked on country music, sorry).

The artist was Randy Travis, and the song was *Three Wooden Crosses*. To me there is a message of salvation in this song. There is also hope for people that many of us may count useless in our society. Even for believers, there is a message for those of us that may be too caught up in this world and have lost sight of our purposes here on earth.

The title of this chapter, in my humble opinion, is directed to one line in the song that says, "It's not what you take when you leave this world behind you, it's what you leave behind you when you go." The Scriptures even say, "Do not lay up for yourselves treasures on earth, where moth and rust destroy and where thieves break in and steal; but lay up for yourselves treasures in heaven, where neither moth nor rust destroys and where thieves do not break in and steal. For where your treasure is, there your heart will be also" (Matthew 6:19-21).

I hate to disappoint you, but there will only be three things in heaven: God, His Word, and His people. There won't be any big fancy homes, careers, cars, money, motorcycles, or bank accounts.

The message I understand from the song is that we should pass on a legacy to others—a legacy of love, hope, and a message of salvation. So then, how should we live? May I say that we should live as if we are going to meet God today? The message that should be on our lips should be the same message that the late beloved pastor Adrian Rogers had on his for his entire ministry: "Come to Jesus."

There are no second chances, friends. There is no reincarnation. There's no such thing as *"everybody gets to heaven"*. There's very little time left of your life to procrastinate. How do I know? Because people die. Do you know when you will die? No. I don't, you don't, nobody does.

The mailman in our neighborhood is a Christian. He does something quite unique, being that he works for the government. He wears something on his uniform that allows him to share his faith. You see, it can't be something like, "ask me about Jesus and I'll tell you." It can't even be the *fish* symbol. He simply wears on his collar a small square pin with two question marks in it. Can you guess what that means?

In case you don't know, here they are. Question number one: *"Have you come to the place in your spiritual life where you know for certain that if you were to die today, you would go to heaven?"* Question number two: *"Suppose you were to die today and stand before God, and He were to say to you, 'Why should I let you into My heaven?' What would you say?"*

Read those two questions again please. Do you know the right answers? Do you really *know for certain* that you're going to heaven when you die? Do you know what you'd say if God asked you *why* He should let you in?

Jesus said this in John 14:6: Jesus said to him, 'I am the way, the truth, and the life. No one comes to the Father except through Me.' He didn't say He was *one* of the ways, but *THE* way!

There may have been *three wooden crosses on the right side of the highway,* but there's only ONE cross that you need in your life, where you can find true life, salvation, and peace everlasting!

AWOL

And I, brethren, could not speak to you as to spiritual people but as to carnal, as to babes in Christ. I fed you with milk and not with solid food; for until now you were not able to receive it, and even now you are still not able; for you are still carnal. For where there are envy, strife, and divisions among you, are you not carnal and behaving like mere men?
1 Corinthians 3:1-3

If you're not familiar with what the acronym AWOL, it is a military term that means: *Absent without (official) leave*. In other words, when you're supposed to be somewhere, such as when roll is taken at a base, and you are unaccounted for, you are considered AWOL. You don't have permission to be absent, no leave, no pass, no reason to be gone. Basically, you're in a lot of trouble with your commanding officer.

When someone enlists in the military, he surrenders certain rights and submits himself to a higher authority under which he is trained and serves. When a person confesses his sins and is saved by grace, he is enlisted in God's army. He surrenders, in this case, ALL his rights to a Higher Authority, not just for a few years according to a contract or agreement, but for the rest of his life.

When I was 17 years old, I confessed to my brother and my parents that I knew I wasn't living as a Christian should. I started going to church. I was baptized. I started attending bible studies, listening to Christian music—as opposed to the secular music that had previously ruled my thoughts—and tried my best to witness to my friends that I used to hang out with and party with.

It wasn't an overnight change, but gradually my life started to look and feel different. I started listening to as much Christian music that *reminded* me of my secular music. I started getting involved with a girl who was not a Christian. I started hanging out with my old friends and not witnessing to them anymore.

In less than two years, you couldn't tell I'd changed one bit. I won't go into details, but I knew I wasn't living right.

If I had been in the military, I would surely have been considered AWOL. I wasn't where I was supposed to be, and I felt like I was under the judgmental hand of God coming to get me and lock me up.

Maybe after you were saved, you didn't go back to your old ways completely like I did (there's more to the story obviously). But have you grown a little cold, or has your passion for sharing with the lost kind of fizzled out? You still go to church, read your bible, and hang out in your Christian circles, but something isn't quite the same. Could you even be like the Christians Paul was writing to that were like *babes?* Could it even be said about you (not that you'd ever admit this), "where there are envy, strife, and divisions among you, are you not carnal and behaving like mere men?" (see 1 Corinthians 3:3) Could you also be AWOL?

Because of how God has worked in my life, I can trace a few years ago where I was when I was struggling, where I wasn't fully surrendered in my heart.

I can look back in my journals and see the hand of God at work leading me and guiding me to be all in, and no longer AWOL. There's a significant difference between the person who just says he is a Christian and the person who lives like it. You might even be shocked at the former person when he says he is a Christian, because until you asked him, nothing in his life showed evidence of it.

It's obvious when you see a person in the military, especially in airports. He has the uniform, he has the haircut, he has the baggage issued by the military—he just looks *military,* he is living out what he signed up for.

Nothing I've ever read in God's word speaks about surrendering your life to Christ our Lord (which means Master, like a military commander), and then living the way you want. It's crazy to think you'd enlist in the military and then go do your own thing and show up for duty a couple times a year.

This is a time for personal reflection. Maybe it's a time to talk to God. Maybe it's time for you to re-engage into what you say you do and surrender your life, your all, to Jesus. You know He's like the father of the prodigal, waiting and watching for you to come home. Won't you come home now? If so, here's a prayer for you to use as your re-enlistment prayer, no longer be AWOL from God.

Abba Father,

I'm sorry for not living like I know You want me to. I'm sorry I've forgotten my First Love and started acting like the fool I once was before I knew You. Because I know in my heart that You love me and that You sent Jesus to die and pay for my sins, I ask that You restore me back into Your service, and that I would listen and obey You when You tell me to do what You want me to do. I give myself back to You and ask that Your mercy would overwhelm me to complete surrender once again. I know I'll fail, and I know that each time I do, You'll still be there to pick me up and accept me as a father accepts his child. I ask that You give me a renewed hunger for your word and for fellowship with a body of believers. I pray all these things knowing that You hear my call and know my heart and the words of my prayer. I love you Lord and thank You for what You will do with my life as I surrender it all to You.

Amen

Baby Jesus

For there is born to you this day in the city of David a Savior,
who is Christ the Lord. And this will be the sign to you: You will
find a Babe wrapped in swaddling clothes, lying in a manger.
Luke 2:11-12

I have been involved with prison ministry for about 17 years now. I have many stories I could share about what I've seen over the years, but for now, I'll share just one.

It was almost Christmas, and our team had the privilege of meeting with about a dozen or so inmates one morning. After a brief introduction, we started to sing *Hark the Herald Angels Sing.* In my humble opinion, the men sang wonderfully, and I think it sounded beautiful, considering the acoustical challenges we faced in this all brick room and the lack of musical instruments.

There was one line from that song that stood out to me, and when we'd finished, I made a point to emphasize it.

"Hark the herald angels sing, Glory to the newborn King! Peace on earth and mercy mild, God and sinners reconciled."

Do you see it? I mean, not just the entire line in italics, but the glorious fact of what the birth of Jesus means! *God and sinners reconciled.* Do you understand what that means? There was a huge problem facing mankind that the blood of bulls and goats could never fully satisfy (see Hebrews 10:4). The problem was that sin *separated* us from a righteous and Holy God.

Picture if you will, God on one side of the Grand Canyon and we're on the other side. The only way to reach Him is if that great-divide were accessible by a bridge. Access before Christ came was by faith—many believed in God—and it was credited to them as righteousness (read Romans 4:18-22).

45

What we see clearly in that one line is that, because of the newborn King Jesus, God and sinners were reconciled. That great divide in the Grand Canyon was filled, and we were given access to God by none other than Jesus Christ. He has reconciled us to God. God no longer looks at us as sinners because He sees us through His spotless, sinless Lamb. He has paid the debt we owed by His payment of our sins on the Cross!

Too often we look at the sweet little Baby lying in a manger and stop there. How soon we forget the stench and filth that surrounded Him and His parents who were forced to give birth in such a place. The whole purpose for His coming was to die! He didn't come to be the King that Israel expected. He came to be The King and to fulfill the writings of the Old Testament prophets.

I don't know about you, but it has been my experience that the public in general doesn't have a problem mentioning the name of God, although it is getting a little more hostile. I believe the reason is that *God* to a lot of people is *out there somewhere* (wherever that is) and not as up-close and personal to where He'll interfere with us much.

Now, mention the name of Jesus Christ? Talk about hostile! But leave off the name *Christ* and add the word *baby* at the beginning? Now we simply have a little non-invasive, cuddly little baby in a little manger, a baby that won't do much harm at all—that is if He stays a *baby in a manger*.

Regardless of the time of year you read this, sooner or later you'll need to answer the following question: *"What are YOU going to do with Jesus?"* It is, after all, the most important question in life.

Is He to you a tradition you scarcely celebrate through the hustle and bustle of *getting through* Christmas? Is He just that sweet little baby lying in a manger and nothing more than a passing thought as to His purpose for His birth in the first place? Do you even think about Him at Christmas, or are you just overwhelmed at how many gifts your kids want this year?

Perhaps you believe that the baby did grow up, that he was just a good teacher who eventually made the religious leaders so angry that they put him to death—facts of history, no personal effect on your life, traditions the Christians celebrate but that you don't need.

You may appear like a good person to those around you. You may go to church every Sunday and you may even consider yourself a Christian. After all, your parents were Christians, and you were raised in church, so of course you're a Christian as well, right? Maybe you even prayed and *asked Jesus into your heart* (a man-made phrase, found nowhere in the Word of God).

Please, take a good hard look right now at life and death. Can you look at death and laugh and say to yourself, *"Jesus defeated death on the cross and I do not fear, because I have put my faith in Him alone?"* Or, maybe you're thinking, *"I'm a good person, I believe that Jesus was a baby and then died for my sins."* Believing it and acknowledging it are two opposite sides of the coin. Do you have head knowledge or heart knowledge? Are you trusting in what you have done, or do or do you trust in all that He has done?

Consider this question—what if you were given 6 months to live? Would life and death questions seem important to you then? What then would you think of my question: *What are YOU my friends going to do with Jesus?*

I hate to tell you, but every one of you reading this will die one day. Shouldn't you make certain that you know what you have done with Baby Jesus? Don't waste your life with trivial matters. Live your life for the One that created you and loved you enough to die for you!

Don't waste another second of your life without considering what you need to do. Seek the Lord while He may be found, call upon His Name, confess with your mouth that He is Lord, and turn from your wicked ways. He WILL hear you, He WILL change you from the inside out!

When you face God one day—and you WILL face Him—will He say to you, "Enter the joy of your Lord" (see Matthew 25:21). Or, will He say, "Depart from Me you workers of iniquity" (see Matthew 7:23).

This is my Christmas message for you friends, as odd as it may be. So, I close with one final question: *What are YOU my friends going to do with Jesus?*

Believing A Lie

A faithful witness does not lie, but a false witness will utter lies.
Proverbs 14:5

When a lie is believed long enough, it becomes the truth.

I don't claim to have originated the above statement, although I've heard of it being put in ways much like that. However, if you think about it, there's truth to that statement.

I've never met a single person that says they enjoy being lied to. I have never met a single person that says they enjoy being deceived, and never met a single person that wants to be cheated. Have you?

But every one of us has been lied to, every one of us has been deceived, every one of us has been cheated. Sometimes when it happens, we don't realize it. The subtle lie sounds like the truth, so we believe it. The deception looks or sounds so good, so it must be real. The cheating takes place behind our backs, so we don't realize it.

The reason we are so easily tricked into believing the lies is because they sound so close to the truth.

Now if I told you to give me your address and that I'm going to send you a magic lamp that will grant you three wishes when you rub it, you would laugh at me because you know that's impossible (well, on second thought there may be a few takers out there). Most of you would know I was lying. That happens in fairytales, not real life. That would be far from the truth.

However, if I walked up to you and said that I had some money I wanted to give you as a gift, wouldn't that be much easier to believe? Of course, it would. Money in someone's hand is more believable than a magic lamp, right? Taking it out and handing it to you would really be believable. It would be believable, but only if the money were real. Let me explain.

Here in the U.S. banking industry, and most likely in other parts of the world, one part of a bank teller's training is identifying counterfeit money. Instead of telling them all the various kinds of counterfeit money they might see, they are taught what the genuine, real money looks like. That way when they are counterfeit money, the bank tellers will be able to differentiate it from real money. Because of their training, they know that anything that doesn't look like real money, is fake.

Let's look at something that can teach us more about being careful not to believe a lie.

The Bible says in Genesis 1:1, "In the beginning God created the heavens and the earth." During creation, God created Adam, the first man, and soon after, God created Eve, the first woman, out of man. Everything was perfect. They lived in a perfect place and had a personal, intimate relationship with a perfect God.

Then came the serpent, Satan, who twisted God's words just a little bit. It sounded like the truth, but it was a lie. He planted doubt in their minds. How did he do it? Simply questioning them. He asked, "Did God really say not to eat of every tree of the garden?" Eve should have turned to her husband and asked him what they should do. Or even better, call out to God, "God! This snake is talking about You!" But, she didn't. You wouldn't be reading this if she did the right thing. Her reply? "No, we can eat the fruit, just not the one in the middle of the garden." Then came the big lie when Satan told her his reason why God didn't want them to eat it: "If you eat it, your eyes will be open, and you will become like God" (see Genesis 3:4-5).

It wasn't *very* far from the truth. All he had to do was plant a little doubt in her mind. Satan takes the truth and makes his lies sound so good, as if they were the truth. And the longer you believe lies from the enemy, the longer you will believe it is the truth.

The Bible also warns us about the counterfeiters that seem like real Christians.

Matthew 7:15 says, "Beware of false prophets, who come to you in sheep's clothing, but inwardly they are ravenous wolves." They sound real, and they even come to you, but they are counterfeits.

Jesus tells a parable in Matthew 13:24-30 that further illustrates counterfeits.

"The Kingdom of Heaven is like a farmer who planted good seed in his field. But that night as the workers slept, his enemy came and planted weeds among the wheat, then slipped away. When the crop began to grow, and produce grain, the weeds also grew. "The farmer's workers went to him and said, 'Sir, the field where you planted that good seed is full of weeds! Where did they come from?' "'An enemy has done this!' the farmer exclaimed. "'Should we pull out the weeds?' they asked. "'No,' he replied, 'you'll uproot the wheat if you do. Let both grow together until the harvest. Then I will tell the harvesters to sort out the weeds, tie them into bundles, and burn them, and to put the wheat in the barn.'" (Matthew 13:24-30; NIV)

Satan tries to counterfeit Christianity. He wants to make it look as close as possible to the real thing. He wants people like you and me to think they are going to heaven by simply *doing* things. Satan is not against religion. It's his best tool in sending people to hell.

This is the reason why there so many false religions that look like the real thing. Have you ever noticed that most all false religions are *works based?* What I mean by that is, *you* must do your part for God (or whoever you worship) to do his (or her, or its) part.

Christianity is the *ONLY* true, biblical faith that leaves salvation up to what Jesus did for us on the cross. A bold statement that a lot of other religions don't like is what Jesus said in John 14:6, "I am the way, the truth, and the life..." *the* truth, not a counterfeit.

Pay close attention to what you're reading. There are so many lies out there. What would you rather believe? Those lies? Or would you rather believe in the truth and in the One who is Truth?

The truth is that the Bible says we are all sinners and that the punishment for being a sinner is death, an eternal separation from God, and an eternity in hell.

But there is good news. Jesus, the Son of God, came to this earth, lived a perfect life, and died on the cross to pay for our sins. And then He rose from the grave. He paid the penalty for sin once and for all. *Our* sin. But that doesn't mean that no matter what you do or how you live, your sins are paid for.

The only way we can be saved from hell is to turn from our sins and believe that Jesus is the *ONLY* way to heaven, not one of many ways. Trust Him. He is the Truth. He asks that we believe in our hearts that He lived, that He died, and that He rose again to give us life. "If we confess with our mouths and believe, we will be saved" (see Romans 10:9-10).

Won't you come to Jesus today?

Brownie Recipe

Above all else, guard your heart, for everything you do flows from it.
Proverbs 4:23 (NIV)

I have been accused on more than one occasion of being the kind of person that *thinks outside the box*, which brings up and interesting subject. Where do common, everyday sayings come from? We use them so often but know little about their origins. Take the one I just mentioned, for example. Where did "think outside the box" come from?

Well, "**Thinking outside the box** entails a thinking process, which comprehends the implementation of an unusual approach to the logical thinking structure. It´s a procedure which aims to escape relational reasoning and thinking."[7] So, the bottom line is, I can be a little *unusual* at times, truth be told.

A few other ones I thought I'd mention are: "bite the bullet," "break the ice," "butter someone up," and "cat got your tongue?" Or one I often use, "what's down in the well comes up in the bucket."

That's the one I want to spend a little time on. Read the verse at the top once again. Did you read it? Do you see the correlation? In other words, if your heart is the well, then the water is everything that flows. Get the picture? Here's another verse to put it into perspective. "A good man brings good things out of the good stored up in his heart, and an evil man brings evil things out of the evil stored up in his heart. For the mouth speaks what the heart is full of" (Luke 6:45; NIV). Allow me to illustrate the point further.

A guy that I work with asked me if I'd ever seen a movie that he thought was very good. Not only had I not seen it, I'd never heard of it. I had asked a couple other guys at work who are Christians if they've seen

---

[7] Patricia Alexander as quoted in "Thinking Outside Of The HR Box," newtohr.com/thinking-outside-of-the-hr-box/ (accessed December 6, 2018); emphasis mine.

it, and they said they had. When I asked what it was rated, they didn't know, but they did add by saying, "Oh it's not that bad. It just has a little bad language in it.

So, since the story and the rest of the movie were so highly recommended, I thought I would give it a try and accepted the offer to borrow it. As I started to watch it one night, I only made it about 15 minutes into the movie before I finally had to turn it off. I wasn't sure what I would say or how I was going to explain it to the guy who suggested it to me. I thought he might not understand.

Surprisingly, when I talked with him the next day and told him what had happened, he understood my position completely. He even apologized to me for bringing it up in the first place and giving it to me to watch. This gave me an opportunity to tell him the *why* behind my reason for not wanting to watch it.

This incident reminded me of a story I received via email quite some time ago. Whether it is true or not does not matter. The point is in the story itself. It goes like this:

There was a man who had two teenage daughters. They asked if they could go see a rated PG-13 movie. The dad asked them what it was about and why the PG-13 rating was on it. They replied that there were just a few bad scenes and some bad language, but that the rest of the movie was good. Besides, all their friends had already seen it. The dad decided to let them go to the movie. But before they were to go and see it, the dad made some brownies for them to take along. He described how good they were, what ingredients he used to make them, the finest of everything. But just before they left, he told them *everything* that was in the brownies.

"To the recipe, I added some dog poop, too," he said. "But just a little bit. With all the good stuff in there you'll hardly notice it." Much to his amazement, his daughters understood the point he was trying to make and decided not to go see the movie.

The Bible says, "And do not be **conformed** to this world, but be **transformed** by the renewing of your mind, that you may prove what is that good and acceptable and perfect will of God" (Romans 12:2; emphasis mine).

Don't get me wrong here. I'm not talking about isolation from everything bad in this world. The news, the headlines, the street corners in some places, for that matter, the malls—try spending an hour there where you don't see something that, if you spent enough time dwelling on it, your water would become a little contaminated.

The CMA ministry we're involved in involves reaching out to a lost and dying world. Guess what? They're not in the pews of our churches; they're at the bars and rallies where everything isn't sugar and spice and everything nice.

However, let me be clear. I'm not advocating that every Christian should place himself in areas of temptation. You know your weaknesses brother or sister. You know your past, whether it was tainted with something God delivered you from and whether you should steer clear of that. I can't make that call. That, my dear friends, should be between you and God.

Compromising God's word will never produce an intimate relationship with Him. To keep your water clean, be careful what's in your well, for everything you do (and think) flows from it. Just like the brownie recipe, the *good* mixed with the *not good* never makes it acceptable.

Building Bridges

So then neither he who plants is anything, nor he
who waters, but God who gives the increase.
1 Corinthians 3:7

Mission trips—eye opening, life changing, perspective altering. Those are just a few ways I would describe them. They are certainly not a foreign concept in the eyes of the church, or for that matter, since the time of the Apostles. Jesus sad, "Go therefore and make disciples of all the nations, baptizing them in the name of the Father and of the Son and of the Holy Spirit, teaching them to observe all things that I have commanded you; and lo, I am with you always, even to the end of the age" (Matthew 28:19-20).

We call that the *Great Commission.* Tragically, today it's also the greatest *omission.* In the verses above, Jesus commanded us to *go... make disciples... teaching them... because He is with us.* In our daily routines, as we're going about our day, we are to make disciples, who prior to that, were new converts. We had to share the gospel with them (maybe we watered, maybe we planted) so they confessed Jesus as Lord and believed in His Name—ONLY because the Holy Spirit transformed them! Now they are ready to learn, to be discipled.

God is at work in the entire process, not us. He gives the talents and abilities. He enables us. He gives us the Holy Spirt to do what He wants. It is by His sovereignty that He places us when and where He wants, to use us, all to bring glory to Him.

How is it done on the mission field? Jeff and Karen Thomas, missionaries with the IMB[8], can tell you. I saw it take place firsthand on one of the international trips I was on in Guatemala. The church I was attending at the time sent a team to Guatemala with a purpose in mind: that the door of opportunity would be opened to share the gospel with

---

[8] International Mission Board (imb.org).

the lost people, by building *bridges.* In my humble opinion, Jeff and Karen have the *Great Commission* figured out.

Our goal for the week was to build *stoves* (not bridges) in homes of the Pokomchi.[9] In other words, the *bridges* that needed to be built were filling the *gap* in the trust relationship that Jeff and Karen needed to be able to share the gospel more effectively.

The purpose of the stove project was to help the people have a more effective way to cook. What they had been accustomed to was causing harm to those in the homes. Smoke and ash would fill the homes up to the ceilings and after a while, it grew into a thick tar-like substance they breathed every day.

Compared to most of us, they have practically nothing. Despite that, they are the hardest working people I've ever seen. Although our cultures differ, they, like us, are just people, too. They work, they eat, they sleep, they have kids, and they live and die just like you and me.

In another way, they are like us, too. They worship. However, not always the same way, and not always the same God. Their hearts and minds have been deceived by the enemy to believe there are many gods—gods that live in the mountains that need human sacrifices (not what first comes to your mind). Shortly before we came there, a landslide took 120 lives. Some felt the *gods* took them as a *human* sacrifice. They have little gods in their homes on their tables too, gods that are never fully satisfied with what they do, so they must keep trying harder to be better.

Jeff and Karen began to see how the hearts of the people were more receptive to hearing the gospel than ever before, simply by our team building the stoves. We also had the opportunity to tell Bible stories

---

[9] According to Jeff Thomas, this is the traditional spelling. Compare: *Wikipedia, The Free Encyclopedia,* s.v. "Poqomchi'_people," (accessed December 6, 2018), https://en.wikipedia.org/wiki/Poqomchi'_people

and to pray with them and for them before we moved on to the next home.

At the end of the week, and 67 stoves later, the gospel message of hope was presented to hundreds of lives that beforehand, kept their distance from the Thomas's.

Jeff shared with our team just before we'd left that he was invited back to the village we worked in to start a Bible study in one of the homes! That was unheard of a week before we had arrived. Praise Almighty God!

You may not have the opportunity to travel internationally, but you can still do the work of a missionary. Where? Right where your sphere of influence is, with your neighbors, your friends, your co-workers, those in the stores you go, and those in the *highways and byways* as Jesus did (see Luke 14:23).

You may not think you can. You may compare yourselves with missionary greats or with pastors, gifted speakers, seminary trained people, or anyone that has a knack at sharing the gospel effectively. But if you do, you'll never measure up and give up. Yet you can share the *Good News* simple by telling *your story.* People may argue with a lot of theological ideas, but they can never argue with you based on how you came to Christ as Lord of your life. Just tell them who you were before... and who you are now.

Now that is a *bridge* you can *build* whoever you are, wherever you are.

Catastrophic Copies

Beloved, do not believe every spirit, but test the spirits
to see whether they are from God, because many
false prophets have gone out into the world.
1 John 4:1 (NASB)

Although she may not come right out and label me a 'pack-rat,' I'll almost bet you that's what she thinks about all the things I save. Okay, so maybe I save a little more than the average person, but hey, you never know when you might need that leftover washer to the fan kit that had eleven and required only ten. I have been known to use things like that before. Bless her heart, my wife means well anyway.

Now, the other things she says I save (which are equally worthless in her opinion) are the things that are in fact worth something! She has absolutely no idea that the sets of *The Family Handyman* magazine I have dating back to over 20+ years ago have a huge significant value. Not only that, they are packed full of incredible home project ideas, landscaping tips, plumbing and electrical assistance, and appliance repair pointers, not to mention all the remarkable stories.

It's hard to put a price tag on the values of magazines like that, right? After my female readers peel themselves off the floor and stop laughing, you may read on (I'm sure the men reading this are in 100% agreement with me).

The following story came from one of the magazines I just mentioned. To my recollection, it was submitted, much to his chagrin, by the guy that *attempted* to build this home project.

The story goes that this DIY (do-it-yourself) guy began the project of building a deck on the back of his house. He'd read all the how-to books he needed to successfully build the deck, bought the lumber, poured the footing, and had all the tools necessary to complete the project.

He thought the project was coming together quite nicely, and he was especially proud of himself when his wife checked periodically and said how great the job looked. The next step was to cut the boards for the deck. That should be the easiest part of the project since the boards would all be the same length. He had spared no expense on the lumber, buying the best top of the line wood he could find.

He made his fist cut after measuring it a couple times and checked the fit. Perfect. He measured another board twice (he'd read that is the best thing to do: measure twice, cut once). Measuring each cut twice soon became old and time consuming. He decided the faster thing to do would be to lay the board he just cut on top of the next board, make his pencil mark, cut, and repeat the process. He thought, "I'll have this done in no time at all doing it this way!" Away he went.

After he'd finished cutting all the boards, (which by now should all be the same size, right?), he began nailing them in place. It didn't take long at all before he was puzzled to discover that each time he tried to put the next board in place, it was tighter than the one before. This grew worse and worse until he couldn't get the boards in any longer.

His dilemma was staring at him. "How could it be that I made copies of all these cuts, and none of them fit anymore?" Much to his embarrassment, his wife solved the problem when he had explained his process. She plainly stated, "You can't make copies of copies. You must use the original." She knew this simple fact because she had made several dresses, always using the original pattern to make more. Fortunately, with a lot of work and a lot of measuring, Mr. DIY would be able to correct his mistake since the boards were all cut longer than needed and not shorter.

Did you know Scripture refers to *Catastrophic Copies?* Okay, indirectly it does. We've never been commanded by our Lord to make copies of copies. You know why? If I made a copy of myself, and that copy made another copy, the results would be worse than the Mr. DIY. Before long there would be a bunch of Pharisee's running around!

What exactly did our Lord tell us about *not* making copies? Matthew 28:18-20 says, "Then Jesus came to them and said, 'All authority in heaven and on earth has been given to me. Therefore, go and make disciples [not copies of yourselves] of all nations, baptizing them in the name of the Father and of the Son and of the Holy Spirit, and teaching them to obey everything I have commanded you [*not what copies think they should do*]. And surely, I am with you always, to the very end of the age.'" (NIV; comments in brackets are mine).

Jesus Christ was the exact representation of His Father, in human flesh—100% God and 100% man (see Hebrews 1:3). That is the *original* we're to copy! Not JT Sedory, and not you either, my friends.

Are you wondering where the verse under the chapter title fits in to all this? If you haven't figured it out by now, let me explain. Have you ever noticed what happens when a pastor or leader leaves his ministry? The *sheep* scatter because their *master* has left the flock. What they were following, was a *false copy* made by wrong measuring. That leader everyone thought was the *real thing* led many to believe they needed him to survive. In fact, if we're truly following Jesus Christ as our Lord and Savior, our confidence and hope is in Him and Him alone.

I hope to write much more about discipleship later (another book). Meanwhile, make sure you're *copying* yourself after the original, otherwise there is a catastrophe about to take place.

Death

Yea, though I walk through the valley of the shadow of death, I will fear no evil; For You are with me; Your rod and Your staff, they comfort me.
Psalm 23:4

I can't tell you how many times I've been to visitations and funerals. Honestly, I have no idea, but if I had to guess, it might be well over 25. Our family lost many relatives before I was even 15 years old. In fact, when my Aunt Dorothy died, during my rebellious teen years, I refused to go to her funeral. I guess I had decided I'd seen enough people in coffins at that point. I live with that regret to this day. She lived with us because she barely had the mind of a 10-year-old even though she was 36 when she died.

What about you? Have you experienced the loss of loved ones and friends? Death surrounds us. Death is inevitable for each one of us. Have you ever heard the commercial slogan that goes like this: *four out of five dentists recommend sugarless gum*? Here's another statistic for you: *One out of one people eventually die*. It's the number one thing in life we'd rather not talk about and something we try to cheat as often as we can. But, sooner or later it will happen to everyone.

Just a few days before he died, Dr. Adrian Rogers[10], long-time pastor of Bellevue Baptist Church, spoke these last words to his family regarding death, "This is a win-win situation!" What he meant was, I believe, as Paul said in Philippians 1:21, "For to me, to live *is* Christ and to die *is* gain."

Either way, for Adrian Rogers, it was glorious.

With something as inevitable as death, do you suppose we might want to consider what happens after we die? Is there anything? Or, are

---

[10] *Wikipedia, The Free Encyclopedia*, s.v. "Adrian Rogers," (accessed December 6, 2018), https://en.wikipedia.org/wiki/Adrian_Rogers

you one of those people that believes that once you're dead, you're dust and never exist again? If you believe anything at all about God (and I certainly hope you do), then the bible is no stranger to the subject of death. In fact, the word "death" occurs 395 times in the New King James Version of the bible.

But there's something else that troubles me about death. It's how callous we have become as a society to the insensitivity of it. It's practically on every TV channel, in every movie, makes every headline. It is the topic of the local news every night, social media seems obsessed with it, and video games are packed full of it. The list goes on and on.

I still remember a game I had on my computer back in the early nineties. The goal was to kill your opponents as they came out from around every corner. It was addicting, I must admit. But it became so addicting that I started to lose sleep over it. I'm not kidding you. It came to a point, that when I closed my eyes to go to sleep at night, I would picture that game and killing my victims. It wasn't long before I got rid of that *game*.

What else has changed about how we view death? How about life itself? How about abortion? Oh wait, I mean *pro-choice* to be politically correct. How about euthanasia? Sorry, I did it again, I mean *mercy killing*. That sounds more passionate, right? When did certain people get the idea that they have the right to choose who lives and who dies? Does that not seem a *little* callous towards life? I saw a billboard recently that said, *"Everyone who is for abortion has already been born."* It's called murder in my book! Or better yet, God's book! (see Exodus 20:13).

It is my opinion that over the last 50+ years people have become more and more desensitized to the value of life for several reasons. Although the following are not evil in and of themselves, I believe they've contributed to the downward spiral. How about the Internet? Anything that comes from man's imagination can be found in the privacy of his home on the Internet. I'm talking about evil, sinful things. How about social media? That could be extended to include Facebook, tweets,

Instagram, TV, movies, videos, DVD's, the music industry, magazines, and a myriad of other things. All those can be good, clean, entertaining things, but quite often they are used to be indifferent about the value of life itself.

This isn't a new trend however. Since man has inhabited planet earth (after the fall) there has been jealously, hate and murder. May I remind you the first family had one brother kill another brother.

As I was writing this, yet another tragic event has unfolded, the senseless killing of 58 innocent lives by one sinister man in what is now the single most deadly shooting in history. Callous. Senseless. Brutal. Murder. Before authorities could get to him, this deranged man, took his own life as well. Some may call that justice—saving millions of dollars for his protection while going through the prosecution and prison sentencing. Although you may fully disagree with my opinion, I can only imagine that man burning in hell now even though Jesus willingly took upon Him that man's sin. Remember, our Lord was *not willing that any should perish* (see 1 Peter 3:9).

Somewhere in his life, that man crossed the line, hardened his heart and sold his soul to the devil, and once and for all sealed his own fate by denying the very power that would save him.

I mentioned how many funerals and visitations I've attended in my lifetime. I've attended several more while writing this. The one thing I've heard every time, with one exception, is that everyone that was eulogized were now in heaven. Does that mean *everybody goes to heaven?*

How do they know? Because they were church members? Because they were good people? Because the family told them they were saved once? How about this for an explanation: who would want to go to a funeral where the minister said the person lying in the casket was now burning in hell? The family and those in attendance would tar and feather the guy and burn him at the stake, right?

But is that doing justice? Is that speaking the truth in love? Is that being honest and truthful if in fact those doing the funeral really are believers?

Maybe you're raising an eyebrow and wondering how else this could be done. Let me tell you what I saw at a funeral of one of the employees of the company I work for who was killed in a car accident. His name was Ken, and he was a Vietnam Veteran. I don't know if Ken ever put his faith in Christ. I'd witnessed to him several times. I bought him a bible. I remember going to his apartment once to tell him he had one more chance at work due to his numerous absences from work because of his drinking problem.

The last time I saw him was on a Friday at work, and the last words I spoke to him were my usual invitation to join me at church. Early the next morning, his sister, who lived a couple streets over from me frantically knocked at my door and rang the bell. She told me that Ken was killed early in the early morning hours. His truck had hit a telephone pole and he had been killed instantly. My heart hurt for his sister, and my heart hurt because I honestly didn't know where Ken would spend eternity.

That question wasn't included by the pastor who led Ken's service at the Veterans Cemetery. In fact, he did such an incredible job conducting the service, that I don't think anyone else noticed his transition. He went from taking about Ken's life, his service in the Military, his work career, and his family that was present, to a full gospel message. The focus became those who were still able to decide for Jesus, not on the one who was in the casket.

Contrast this with what I witnessed at a recent funeral. The pastor's sole purpose I believe, was to give the deceased family members and those present, a hope that their loved one was now in the arms of Jesus. He didn't mention it a few times, either. His whole sermon was focused on the one who had died. He spoke of visions he'd had, reassuring every one of the certainties of it. He did give a gospel message at the end, though that was not completely biblical.

Do any of you remember the prayer often taught to children to recite at bedtime? It went like this: *"Now I lay me down to sleep, I pray the Lord my soul to keep: If I should die before I 'wake, I pray the Lord my soul to take."*

As cute as that prayer is, may I suggest you do something before you lie down to sleep tonight? One thing is certain: death. People seldom plan their deaths. Tonight, might be your time. I'm not trying to scare you; I'm simply stating a fact. We just don't know when our time will be. Wouldn't it be wise to say that *you know for sure, beyond a shadow of a doubt, where you will go after you die?*

(See Appendix for more help in knowing the certainty of your eternal home)

Do This in Remembrance

For I received from the Lord what I also passed on to you:
The Lord Jesus, on the night he was betrayed, took bread,
and when he had given thanks, he broke it and said,
"This is My body, which is for you; do this in remembrance of Me."
1 Corinthians 11:23-24 (NIV)

Several years ago, while I was on vacation in California, I saw a prayer request shared on Facebook by a friend from back in Tennessee. All it stated was, *"Pray for Tim Warren and his family."* I initially responded to it by asking, "What's going on with them?" I then realized with the two-hour time difference, as late as it was in CA (after 10:00 pm), I probably wouldn't see a response until the next day. I knew Tim Warren. He was a Memphis Police Officer and a member of the same Christian Motorcyclists Association chapter as me, Wheels of Grace. We were members of the same church, and we were even neighbors—he lived just a couple of blocks away.

I felt bad, but I had not talked with Tim for nearly a month or two, and I wasn't sure why. I really wanted to know why this other friend asked for prayer for him and his family, and I couldn't wait until morning to find out.

I'm not sure what prompted me at that moment (I know now), but I looked up the website for News Channel 3 in Memphis on my phone. The first news story that came up was that "Memphis Police Officer Tim Warren was shot and killed in the line of duty." [11] I was absolutely numb. I couldn't believe what I had read. I was hurting for his family. I told the friends I was staying with that a friend back home had been shot and killed.

---

[11] *Facebook,* "RIP Memphis Police Officer Timothy Warren",
https://www.facebook.com/RememberingOfficerWarren/ (accessed, December 7, 2018).

Shortly after Tim's death, several things were being discussed on social media about his character and who Tim Warren really was. Sometimes that's when skeletons come out of people's past. Not Tim's. People started to learn that he was more than just another cop killed in the line of duty. They learned about his love for the Lord, his love for his brothers and sisters in Christ, his passionate heart and love for his family, and his love for the people he worked among: the helpless, the homeless, and the less fortunate. Even in the last few moments of Tim's life, he was responding to a cry for help. Yes, Tim was a police officer Yes, he was responding to a call. Yes, it was his job. But all I heard afterwards was that it was more than a job to him; it was a tool to reach out and minister to those hurting souls he encountered.

Tim will be remembered for who he was as a father, a husband, a police officer, a friend and a believer in Christ. The very *One* he is worshipping forever. However, none of us that knew Tim are personally trusting that he'll do anything for us anymore, right?

Take Jesus, on the other hand. He is a whole different story — and His story is what transforms our story!

For me, when I take the Lord's Supper, I remember what He did for me on the cross. As I take the bread and the cup, it's a time to remember, to reflect, to confess, and to be thankful that our Lord offered Himself a willing sacrifice for our sins. Breaking the bread, a representation of His body broken for us (see Luke 22:19); drinking the cup to remember what Christ was about to do: shed His perfect blood on our behalf (see Luke 22:20). And this was recorded in Scripture for us: to remember and to do it in remembrance of Him.

But is that all we're to remember about our Savior? What He did? How about what He *is doing?* We're to *remember* what He did to give us *life* in Christ, yet we live expectantly as the Holy Spirit guides us to become more like Jesus through obedience. We do that by the transformation of our minds (see Romans 12:2). We come to the Lord's table to *remember* His death, burial, and resurrection so that we *walk in newness of life* (see Romans 6:4).

When you trust Jesus Christ as your Savior and Lord, and surrender your life to Him, no longer a slave to sin, you, like my friend Tim, will one day be celebrating with Him in Glory.

Easter—The *Real* Pain

Those who passed by hurled insults at him... In the same way,
the chief priests and the teachers of the law mocked him...
Those crucified with him also heaped insults on him.
From Mark 15:29, 31, 32 (NIV)

One of the childhood memories I have about Easter is getting those chocolate Easter bunnies. Some of them were hollow, but the ones I really loved were the solid milk chocolate ones. I hate to admit it, but there were times I got more than one (two sets of grandparents helped) and ate them so fast I'd get sick. I don't know too many kids that don't love chocolate.

As a kid, Easter was a special day to me only because I got some candy. Plus, I knew it was different because I usually got a new set of clothes to wear to church. That, and our church and family gatherings, were different than most other Sundays. I sure I heard about Jesus and the cross and the resurrection, but apparently it never made an impact on me back then.

As an adult, Easter began to take on an entirely different meaning. I still had much to learn, and I still don't think I fully appreciated what it cost our Lord, until a few years ago, when I saw a movie depicting his suffering.

You may have seen the movie *The Passion of the Christ*[12] directed by Mel Gibson. It was while I was watching that movie for the first time that I realized just how much God loved me and just how much Jesus really suffered on my behalf. There is no conceivable way an average man could have endured what He did.

In that movie, the physical suffering that our Lord endured, which, by the way, is described in His word (see John chapter 19), is emphasized

---

[12] *Wikipedia, The Free Encyclopedia*, s.v. "The Passion of the Christ," (accessed December 7, 2018), https://en.wikipedia.org/wiki/The_Passion_of_the_Christ

and depicted above all other circumstances that took place. But I'd like to suggest to you, something you may not have thought about before. I think His *pain* was three-fold. But, there was a purpose in the pain. All the pain. Doesn't our God always have a purpose (see Romans 8:28)?

The Bible says that Jesus was "...the Lamb who was slain from the creation of the world" (Revelation 13:8b; NIV). Don't glance over that too quickly. It says, "from the creation of the world." Have you ever entertained the thought that Jesus coming to die was God's Plan B after sin got so bad and entered the world? Wrong. It was His plan of redemption from creation.

Don't lose your mind trying to figure out God's plan with that. You'll sleep much better at night if you really trust that He has a perfect plan and that He knows what He's doing. Isaiah 55:9 says, "As the heavens are higher than the earth, so are my ways higher than your ways and my thoughts than your thoughts"(NIV).

What about the sin that Jesus was about to take to the cross? On top of the physical pain He suffered, He knew what He was about to suffer on the cross — paying a debt that mankind could never pay. He sweat drops of blood in the Garden of Gethsemane asking God to remove the cup of suffering he was about to *drink* (see Matthew 26:39, Luke 22:44). But He also prayed, "not My will, but Yours, be done" (Luke 22:42).

So, we read about and see the physical pain, and we know about the pain of bearing the sin of the world. What about the third type of pain He suffered? I hope you never lose sight of who Jesus really was. He was the only God-Man. So, he was God in human flesh, but He was a man too.

I think the pain we overlook is Jesus' broken heart. Think about it. He went through emotional pain from those He loved.

All of us have experienced physical pain in our lives. We've all been sick, some have had broken bones, some have had lingering illnesses, and some of us have had serious accidents All of these things hurt physically. Now think about a pain inflicted from a friend or family member that really broke your heart. I mean it really, really hurt. Maybe you're thinking about that person right now and it still hurts as you feel the pain from that relationship.

Now think about Jesus on the night when He was arrested, from the moment Judas kissed Him to identify Him to the angry mob. He loved the centurions that arrested Him and led Him to His mock trial. He loved the ones that spit on Him, the ones that beat Him, the one that placed the crown of thorns on His head, and the ones that made Him carry His cross. He loved the ones that scourged Him, and He loved the people in the streets that yelled and mocked Him as He was led to Calvary. He loved the soldiers that beat Him mercilessly, He loved the ones that drove the nails in His hands and feet on the cross, and He even loved the soldier that pierced His side with a spear after He had died.

If that doesn't at least make you become teary-eyed and hurt inside with mixed emotions of sorrow, yet thankfulness for what Christ did for you and for me as He was led to Calvary, then may I suggest you check your pulse?

Better yet, if it has brought you to have a heart of repentance, realizing what Jesus did for you, maybe it's time to fall to your knees and pray, asking the Savior to forgive your sins once and for all (see 1 John 1:9).

Expectations

If you need wisdom, ask our generous God, and he will give it to you. He will not rebuke you for asking. But when you ask him, be sure that your faith is in God alone. Do not waver, for a person with divided loyalty is as unsettled as a wave of the sea that is blown and tossed by the wind. Such people should not **expect** to receive anything from the Lord.
James 1:5-7 (NLT; emphasis mine)

We all have expectations, don't we? No matter where you come from, no matter where you live, young or old, male or female, we all do certain things, interact in certain ways, and basically live day in and day out with expectations. Let me further explain.

Most of our expectations are ones we seldom give a second thought to. They happen from the moment we open our eyes in the morning until we close them to go to sleep. It's the idea that things will happen in a certain way and people will act and react in the way we expect them to It's a given, or so we think. The definition alone would indicate that it's human nature to live this way.

Expectation is: "a strong belief that something will happen or be the case in the future."[13]

Most of that sounds positive, right? But a pessimist with his negative way of thinking, like Eeyore in *Winnie the Pooh and a Day for Eeyore*, can even say, "Good afternoon, Piglet, *if it is a good afternoon, which I doubt.*"[14]

Allow me to give you a few examples that illustrate the thought behind our expectations.

---

[13] Google Search. Google Dictionary. 12 December 2018. Web.
[14]*Wikiquote*, s.v. "*Winnie the Pooh and a Day for Eeyore,*" (accessed December 7, 2018), https://en.wikiquote.org/wiki/Winnie_the_Pooh_and_a_Day_for_Eeyore (emphasis mine).

When we put the key in the ignition of our car, we expect it to start. When we put the key in the front door of our house, we expect it to open. When we turn on a light, a computer, or a cell phone, we expect it to turn on. When we go to work and do our job, we expect our boss to give us a paycheck at the end of the pay period.

We've been programmed from birth and trained our whole lives to have certain expectations in life.

We understand the law of action and reaction: "For every action, there is an equal and opposite reaction."[15] A baby learns that by crying, it can be fed, held, or changed. We understand early and have expectations.

When we were children growing up, we quickly learned from the time we were toddlers that there was something called a rewards system. If you study, you receive good grades. If you receive good grades, you eventually received a diploma. If you had that diploma, you get to graduate. It's engrained in us from the time we are young and all throughout our adult lives. I'm sure you'd agree by now expectations are a way of life.

Therefore, since all human beings are wired to have expectations, we also have certain expectations about God. Agree or disagree?

Keep in mind that we're programmed to expect things. Don't we expect things to go well in life if we are basically good and not hurting anyone? Like *good karma*[16] as a lot of people believe? Or if we care for the widow and the orphan (see James 1:27), shouldn't we somehow be rewarded with a problem-free life? Maybe if we go to church occasionally (or even every Sunday) and are *good and do good*, that should be enough, right?

---

[15] Sir Isaac Newton, Newton's Third Law of Motion.
[16] *Karma*, in both Hinduism and Buddhism, is the sum of a person's actions in this and previous states of existence, viewed as deciding their fate in future existences.

Once again, I say, we all have expectations. If we live by the Golden Rule,[17] then we *expect* to be treated well by others and even by God. At the end of our lives, after we've lived to a ripe old age, and we're surrounded by all our loved ones, we *expect* to take a deep breath, go to sleep, and *expect* to awake in heaven. After all, we've been *pretty good, right?*

I hate to disappoint you, but God does not grade on a curve. There should be no expectations on your destiny if all you've done in life is trying to be a good person. Even if your good outweighs your bad, it won't be *deserved* when it comes to eternal life by *works* (see Ephesians 2:8-9).

Salvation is by grace alone, through the shed blood of Jesus Christ on the cross for the forgiveness of sins (see Ephesians 1:7). Salvation happens when you "confess with your mouth the Lord Jesus and believe in your heart that God has raised Him from the dead" (see Romans 10:9).

If we turn from our sins and follow Him, then—and only then— can we have one *expectation:* that by this act of faith, we will live with Him forever.

Your *expectation* can be a guarantee when it's a promise from Him: "My soul, wait silently for God alone, For my expectation is from Him" (Psalm 62:5).

---

[17] The Golden Rule or Law of Reciprocity is the principle of treating others as one would wish to be treated.

Fatal Distractions

Watch and pray, lest you enter into temptation.
The spirit indeed is willing, but the flesh is weak.
Matthew 26:41

One day as I was leaving for work, I observed something peculiar happening just ahead. There were two robins flying around about eye level, moving very fast and flying practically in circles. They were either chasing each other, playing games with each other, or fighting. Obviously, I wasn't sure.

As many of you know, most *bird* encounters, whether they happen when you're on a motorcycle or in a vehicle, can turn out to be very close and on occasion you may even hit them. In this case, it was the latter of the two. I thought for sure they'd see me coming and fly out of the way. Were they oblivious to my approach? Could they not have waited until I passed by to take up their little game or fight?

I wasn't going that fast at all, and my instinct as I saw them getting too close, caused me to swerve a little at the last minute. But, as I passed by them, I noticed in my rear-view mirror what I was afraid I was going to see, one dead bird lay in the middle of the street.

I had obviously not hit the other bird, because it was standing in the street. I wondered why it was right next to the dead one? I wondered if it did get bumped perhaps by the one now laying there or even part of my vehicle. Is it possible that it stopped to see what happened to the other bird? I believe it did.

For some odd reason, it took me a long time afterwards not to think about those two birds. The scenario kept playing over again in my mind. Then I realized why.

That very same situation for the birds is what happens with people. Think about it for a minute. We can get so easily caught up in what we're doing whether it's running around in circles or chasing and pursuing wrong things (or even people). It could also be playing games when we shouldn't, or even worse, fighting and bickering with one another so much that sometimes we don't see the obvious dangers in our lives headed straight our way.

Have you ever been out driving, riding, running, or just enjoying the outdoors and before you knew it, there was an obstacle you had to overcome ASAP or else? How about the deer that came from out of nowhere? Or the obstacle course of potholes you had to avoid? Or the car that suddenly came into your path? A fallen tree limb? A dog chasing you?

There are plenty of other reasons. How about being so busy at work or with other things that we ignore our families. Or not preparing for the future in the event we get hurt and can't work. Or even a call from the doctor with the shocking news. There are things in life we just can't see coming. Death is like that, too. Even though we hate to think about it, our *vehicle* may be just around our corner just like for those birds.

The bible says, "See then that you walk circumspectly, not as fools, but as wise, redeeming the time, because the days are evil" (Ephesians 5:15-16). The word *circumspectly* means to be watchful and discreet, cautious, and even prudent. The chances of you being blind-sided by sin won't as easily overtake you, *if* you are following the Scriptures instruction.

There's another fatal distraction common among men in particular: women. Most of the time, the temptations that plague us as men are other women we know. I won't spend too much time on this: it's a subject for a future book. But I'll say this: guard your relationships, whether you're a man or a woman, or the fatal distractions are sure to take place (see 1 John 2:15-16).

I will say one more thing before leaving the subject. Think for just a minute how many people you personally know that were married, but because of an affair (adultery), they divorced and married the one they had been involved with. Christian or not, it happens with church members as much as outside the church. Those are fatal distractions that are the biggest problem facing the American family today.

What does the bible say to counteract that type of fatal distraction? That sin? Just one of many verses that may save your life is found in Deuteronomy 5:33: "You shall walk in all the ways which the LORD your God has commanded you, that you may live and that it may be well with you, and that you may prolong your days in the land which you shall possess."

Free Samples

Oh, taste and see that the LORD is good;
Blessed is the man who trusts in Him!
Psalm 34:8

Do you remember any popular advertising slogans from the past? How about these? When you hear, *"I can't believe I ate the whole thing!"* what do you think about? What else but Alka-Seltzer. How about the famous *"Think outside the bun"* slogan? Taco Bell, of course. Then there is the *"Just Do It"* by none other than Nike. And one more: *"Have it your way"* by Burger King. As good as those slogans are (and there are hundreds of them), I like the one that came out many years ago. You most likely saw it on bumper stickers, key chains, t-shirts and bracelets. It was all over. It was simply 4 letters: *WWJD* (What Would Jesus Do). Sounds like a good question for all Christians to ask themselves, doesn't it?

Several years ago, I was hanging out with a friend of mine at a McDonald's. We were talking about how he got hooked on a specialty drink they have. That is what gave me the idea for this chapter. I remembered once when McDonald's first came out with their chicken strips. They gave away samples, so you would buy more. Bright idea, right? The same thing happened when they introduced their oatmeal. I had a *free* coupon, so I tried it. Guess what? I started to buy it because I liked it. I may have never tried it if not for that coupon. And what about food-courts in malls? Walk by anywhere they sell Oriental food and you'll see a guy leaning over the counter with a tasty sample on a toothpick wanting you to try it, so you'll buy more.

By now you're probably wondering, *what's all this talk about advertising and eating?* The Bible says in Psalm 34:8a, "Taste and see that the LORD is good..." No, we're not in the business of selling the Gospel. In fact, you can't buy it. But let me ask you this: *how are people that are lost and destined for hell ever going to come to Jesus if we don't let them know that it (eternal life) is a gift of God?* I must constantly ask myself if I am *good advertising* or *bad advertising* for Jesus. Am I being a beacon of light or am turning people away from Him?

What type of a statement do you make with your life? Are you proud to put it on display? Is your life a *slogan* for Jesus that people will remember and have a hunger for, enough so that they *taste and see for themselves* that the Lord is good (see also 1 Peter 2:2-3)? Oh, how that is *my prayer,* that I am attracting others rather than turning them off to the message of hope and eternal life.

If you have any doubt about what I'm saying, look up the following verses and see what Scripture says our conduct is supposed to be like:

Matthew 5:16, Ephesians 5:1, 1 Corinthians 11:1, Ecclesiastes 12:13, 1 Corinthians 10:31.

Lastly, I want to share a few words from a song written by Melody Green and sung by her late husband, Keith Green,[18] Christian singer, musician, and songwriter, who went home to be with Jesus, on July 28th, 1982. The song Keith sang is called *Make My Life a Prayer to You*, and I highly encourage you to search for the words and listen to the song as well. It begins, *"Make my life a prayer to you, I wanna do what you want me to"* (emphasis mine).

---

[18] *Wikipedia, The Free Encyclopedia*, s.v. "Keith Green," (accessed December 7, 2018), https://en.wikipedia.org/wiki/Keith_Green

Getting There

Thomas said to him, "Lord, we don't know where You are going, so how can we know the way?" Jesus said to him, "I am the way, the truth, and the life. No one comes to the Father except through Me.
John 14:5-6

I really enjoy taking a long, carefully-planned ride on my motorcycle. So far, the farthest I've ridden by myself round-trip is nearly 1300 miles. The other long-distance trip I make annually is only about 600 miles round-trip. These trips would have been epic failures had I not carefully planned them before heading out.

The second time I went on the shorter of these trips, an unplanned detour took place. I had practically memorized the map at the time or, so I thought. But after an hour or so, it was obvious to me and the friends following me that we were lost. Somehow, I had taken a wrong turn, and we needed to know how to get back to where we were, so we could reach our destination.

However, something very cool happened on that detour (I call it a *God-thing,* though some argue using that terminology). We had stopped at a gas station for directions, where we *coincidently* encountered a young mother in the parking lot desperately trying to get into her car. She had come to get something for her little girl, who was sick and asleep in the back seat. She'd left the car running and didn't realize the keys were locked in the car until she came back. Nobody else was there to help her except six lost bikers trying to find their way back to the right road.

It pays to know where you're going, and how to get there, whether it's a short trip or a destination hundreds of miles from home. But travel often enough, and even the best navigator will get lost, if not slightly off course now and then.

Here's some practical advice I try to follow when traveling.

First, plan-ahead as much as possible. Second, know the route you'll take. Third, prepare yourself physically and mentally.

When I plan, I already know the destination before I leave. I have reservations, or I'll be staying with someone. If you don't have a plan and you get somewhere you didn't have a place to stay, you may be sleeping under the stars.

Knowing the route is essential—especially if there may be any detours. In addition to plan stops for fuel, food and sightseeing, just to name a few.

Third, I prepare myself for the trip. Traveling can be strenuous, especially with traffic and construction, or just long distances. It takes a lot of mental preparation and physical rest before you leave.

With today's technology, we seldom use the *old-style fold out maps* (no offense if you still do). It's hard to believe they're practically extinct, isn't it? Yes, you can still find them, but they are not readily available like they used to. People needed them—even depended on them— because they were the *only* way to know where you were going.

Today, we have the Internet, GPS systems, and it seems as if nearly everyone has a smart phone these days that can navigate the user to just about any destination. Yet, even with the best tools available, is it still possible to get lost? Certainly.

If you are given a wrong address, be-it on purpose, or by mistake, will you reach your destination? Not quite. Perhaps in due time after you realize the mistake. What if the tool you're using to travel (map, Internet directions, GPS, etc.) is not up-to-date? Will you still get there? It's doubtful, at least not without serious delays.

Whether you travel a lot or a little or not at all, there's one trip in the future that we'll *all* eventually take, and it's the most important trip of our lives. It's the trip we'll take when we die. It's most critical to plan for this trip, because this is a One-Way trip you'll never come back from.

Here's some practical advice you should take quite seriously about this eternal trip.

First, plan-ahead as much as possible (sound familiar?). It is an absolute certainty that, unless the Lord comes back for His church (see 1 Thessalonians 4:13-18), you will die one day. And according to Hebrews 9:27, "And as it is appointed for men to die once, but after this the judgment."

It would also be wise of you to find out if you have *reservations* and not just *assume* that you do. I fear many well-meaning, *morally-good* people—even Christian workers in the church—are going to be shocked when they die and stand before the Lord (read Matthew 25:31-46). I pray that you know beyond a shadow of doubt that you have a place prepared for you (see John 14:1-4).

Second, make sure you know the *right way* to get there. Instead of using a man-made GPS, why not use the perfect heavenly-made one— God's GPS: *God's Positioning System; a*lso known as His word. With so many religions in our world today, how can you know the right one? I challenge you to discover the foundation of that religion you're putting hope in. If it's not the one the bible teaches, is it founded on a man? Or is it founded in the God that made man? The bible stands true in so many ways (see several other chapters on the subject).

Third, do what you can to prepare for this trip. Are you abiding with Christ? (see John 15:1-11). Are you keeping His commandments? (see John 14:15). Are you making disciples? (see Matthew 28:19-20).

As mentioned with the car or motorcycle trip, traveling can be strenuous, and in the case of life, it can be overwhelming at times. Sickness, accidents, divorce, tragedy, death—we are not immune to any of it. Our only *Hope* is Jesus Christ to carry us through.

Consider these words you've just read carefully my friends. If the truth of eternal life were a certainty, wouldn't you want to know about it? See 1 John 5:13. Make sure you know the *right* way to get there. That is my plea to you. Many people have claimed over the years to know the way. They even say that there are many ways to get to Heaven. But Jesus said in John 14:6, "I am the way, the truth, and the life." Prepare yourself. Never put it off until tomorrow. You May never get a *tomorrow.* The Bible says, "now is the day of salvation" (see 2 Corinthians 6:2).

Hebrews 11 & 12

Now faith is the substance of things hoped for,
the evidence of things not seen.
Hebrews 11:1
Therefore we also, since we are surrounded by
so great a cloud of witnesses...
Hebrews 12:1a

Several years ago, when I lived in California, I wanted a career change, and began to pursue law enforcement. Part of that pursuit was in getting some *on the job training.* This training wasn't through official channels, but instead consisted of spending some time in a patrol car with a good friend who worked for the department. I rode with him during his shift (which was 3:00 pm to 1:00 am, sometimes later) perhaps a dozen times. I'll save the stories for some other time (there were some good, and some bad).

One thing I learned on those rides, as well as through studying law enforcement books, is about evidence. One key is that you don't mess with evidence. The other is that when trying to prove a case, you need evidence.

But is the foundation of Christianity the same? Can anyone show their faith? Can anyone see God? Can anyone see Jesus in bodily form or see the Holy Spirit? All those things will take faith!

Please don't take that the wrong way. In no way am I trying to get you to doubt anything, especially your faith. Just because you don't have proof of ALL the things I just mentioned, there is no reason to doubt God or His word. My faith in God is based on what He has done with me! He took a good-for-nothing sinner like me, transformed me, and forgave me! He translated me out of darkness into His marvelous light! I am now the righteousness of God in Christ Jesus! (see 1 Peter 2:9, 2 Corinthians 5:21).

My life verse is Hebrews 12:1-2. I absolutely love explaining it in detail to people when I have a chance to speak about it. I compare the *great cloud of witnesses* as a large stadium packed with those ready to watch as we *run the race.* They're cheering us on to run *with endurance.* There are so many cases in God's word where those *witnesses* walked by faith. Let's look at just a few.

By an act of faith, the children of Israel walked through the Red Sea on dry ground. The Egyptians tried it and drowned. By an act of faith, the Israelites marched around the walls of Jericho for seven days, and the walls fell flat. And by an act of faith, during that same time, Rahab, the Jericho harlot, welcomed the spies and escaped the destruction that came on those who refused to trust God. By and act of faith, David trusted God and faced Goliath with the odds stacked against him. He believed God would give him victory. By an act of faith, Peter, when he preached to a huge crowd on the day of Pentecost, exercised his faith, and as a result, "three thousand souls were added to them." (see Acts 2:41).

I could go on, but I think you get my point. It's about faith. There are so many more stories of acts of faith mentioned: Gideon, Barak, Samson, Jephthah, David, Samuel, the prophets. Through acts of faith, they toppled kingdoms, made justice work, took the promises for themselves. They were protected from lions, fires, and sword thrusts. They turned disadvantage to advantage, won battles, routed alien armies. Women received their loved ones back from the dead. There were those who, under torture, refused to give in and go free, preferring something better: resurrection. Others braved abuse and whips, and, yes, chains and dungeons. We have stories of those who were stoned, sawn in two, and murdered in cold blood. There are stories of vagrants wandering the earth in animal skins, homeless, friendless, and powerless.

Not one of these people, even though their lives of faith were exemplary, got their hands on what was promised. God had a better plan, that their faith and our faith would come together to make one completed whole—our lives of faith not complete apart from theirs.

Do you see what this means? All these pioneers of faith who blazed the way, all these veterans cheering us on? It means we'd better get on with it. Strip down, start running, and never quit! No extra spiritual fat, no parasitic sins. Keep your eyes on Jesus, who both began and finished this race we're in. Study how He did it. Because He never lost sight of where He was headed. He could put up with anything along the way: the cross, the shame, everything. And now He's there, in the place of honor, right alongside God. When you find yourselves weakening in your faith, go over that story again, item by item, that long litany of hostility He plowed through. That will shoot adrenaline into your souls!

In this all-out match against sin, others have suffered far worse than you, to say nothing of what Jesus went through—all that bloodshed! So, don't feel sorry for yourselves. Run the race with endurance...and keep your eye's *fixed on Jesus!*

Hypocrites are Everywhere

Or how can you say to your brother, 'Brother, let me remove the speck that is in your eye,' when you yourself do not see the plank that is in your own eye? Hypocrite! First remove the plank from your own eye, and then you will see clearly to remove the speck that is in your brother's eye.

Luke 6:42

I have been a believer long enough to know that while you're alive, you will have *issues* from time to time with others. I am not going to beat around the bush in this chapter I'm going to tell it like it is.

Legalism is a trap that is easy to fall into. Let me begin by asking you a few questions. Examine your heart carefully, friends, as you answer these. Have you ever judged someone for something you knew you were guilty of? Do you look at the faults of others, Christian or not, while not giving a second thought to your own faults (see Matthew 7:3)? Have you ever pointed the finger at other people's mistakes only to find yourself doing the same thing?

Okay, in all honesty, did you answer YES to all the questions? To those of you that *may* have answered NO to any or all them, here's what you need to do. Put this book down and stop reading. Next, call your church and tell them you decided to stop attending because the church is full of hypocrites! Then lock yourself inside your home and don't ever come out. Unplug your phone, TV, computer, anything that will give you access to another human being!

Are you with me? Believe it or not, there are sinners sitting next to you every Sunday morning. In fact, one occupies the seat you and I sit in as well. Oh my, not sinners you say? Yes! But that is no reason to check out. The church is not for perfect people. The church is the body of Christ anyway, and we are imperfect people. "But, thanks be to God, who gives us the victory through our Lord Jesus Christ" (1 Corinthians 15:57).

I have had people tell me to my face that they don't need to go to church to be a Christian. Okay, there's some truth to that. However, some use the *"there's nothing but a bunch of hypocrites there, and the pastor is the worst one"* excuse. That doesn't hold water, friends. That's as bad as refusing to use money because you know there are counterfeit bills floating around, and you wouldn't want to accidentally get any.

We don't quit church because we see another sinner there and we don't stop using money either.

So, what can we do? Remember, I said while you're alive, you'll have *issues* (problems, judging, finger-pointing, unforgiveness) with others. I jokingly tell my friends, *"You know what the problem is with churches today (*substitute the word church with any organization where people are*)? People! How do I know that? Cuz I is one!"*

Back to the question of what we can do. There's a nugget of God's word I found years ago that I taught in a class at my church, calling it *"A Christian's Blueprint Toward One Another."* I base it on the passage below. As you read it (and hopefully you will commit this section of Scripture to memory), think about problems that come up in your church, and ask yourself if the problem would still exist if these principles were applied.

> *Let* love *be* without hypocrisy. Abhor what is evil. Cling to what is good. [10] *Be* kindly affectionate to one another with brotherly love, in honor giving preference to one another; [11] not lagging in diligence, fervent in spirit, serving the Lord; [12] rejoicing in hope, patient in tribulation, continuing steadfastly in prayer; [13] distributing to the needs of the saints, given to hospitality.
> [14] Bless those who persecute you; bless and do not curse.
> [15] Rejoice with those who rejoice, and weep with those who weep. [16] Be of the same mind toward one another. Do not set your mind on high things, but associate with the humble. Do not be wise in your own opinion.
> [17] Repay no one evil for evil. Have regard for good things in the

sight of all men. [18] If it is possible, as much as depends on you, live peaceably with all men. [19] Beloved, do not avenge yourselves, but *rather* give place to wrath; for it is written, "Vengeance *is* Mine, I will repay," says the Lord. [20] Therefore, "If your enemy is hungry, feed him; If he is thirsty, give him a drink; For in so doing you will heap coals of fire on his head." [21] Do not be overcome by evil, but overcome evil with good. (Romans 12:9-21)

Jesus was critical to point out the faults of the Pharisee's and the *muckety-mucks* of His day, because although they knew the Truth, they acted pompous and hypocritical of anyone that didn't look like them and act like them. I wonder what Jesus would say if he walked our streets today? I wonder if He'd even go to our churches to hang out with Christians. Or, would He be on the streets with the sinners like He was when He walked and lived among them? I think we both know the answer to that.

I'll be perfectly honest with you, it's much easier for me to have a critical spirit than a spirit of love and acceptance. It's easier for me to point out faults of others as if I've been appointed to the *plank-patrol watch.* That is my sinful nature rearing its ugly head when I need to allow the Holy Spirit to rule and reign constantly. It's a moment by moment decision we must consciously make to combat the temptation to give the evil one a foothold in our lives.

The next time we're tempted to be a hypocrite and point out our brother's plank, remember that we should "Rather, clothe yourselves with the Lord Jesus Christ, and do not think about how to gratify the desires of the flesh" (Romans 13:14; NIV).

It's A Wonderful Life

You will show me the path of **life**; In Your presence is fullness of joy;
At Your right hand are pleasures forevermore.
Psalm 16:11 (Emphasis mine)

I hope the first thing that comes to your mind after reading the title, is the 1946 movie with Jimmy Stewart and Donna Reed.[19] How many times have you seen it? I make it a point to watch it every Thanksgiving and maybe even the week of Christmas. I watch it while getting ready for the Christmas season because it reminds me just how great a gift *life* really is.

The guardian angel Clarence asked George once, *"You see George, you really have had a wonderful life. Don't you see what a mistake it would be to just throw it away?"* If you've seen the movie, you may not think George had such a wonderful life in comparison to the world's standards. George lived a very simple lifestyle. In fact, he never did get to leave Bedford Falls.

How about you? Do you feel as if your life doesn't count? Like George, have you ever said maybe everyone would be better off if you'd never been born? He didn't feel like he made much of a difference, but oh how wrong he was. Just one life, and yet he touched so many. Just like your life, and mine. We make a difference.

I can guarantee you according to God's word, you are no mistake. You have been fearfully and wonderfully made and God loves you (see Psalm 139).

In this life, there are many opportunities to make a difference. And it doesn't take something BIG to make that difference. It could be that someone you see during the day just needs to see a smile or hear a

---

[19] *Wikipedia, The Free Encyclopedia*, s.v. "It's a Wonderful Life," (accessed December 7, 2018), https://en.wikipedia.org/wiki/It's_a_Wonderful_Life

word of appreciation. Maybe someone you never even know needs someone to talk with or needs someone to pray for them. We will never really know the full impact of our *ministry* this side of glory.

I recently had some other thoughts about life after attending a visitation for a young man—just 22 years old—who had been killed by a drunk driver in a motorcycle accident. Many would say—and I would have to agree—he was too young to die. Cut short. It's over. No more chances to make a difference. The dash after his date of birth now had another date following. As a stranger (I didn't personally know him or his family), it's quite mind boggling to think about.

But one of the things that made my heart ache for the family is that I had not seen on the young man's Facebook page or heard anyone speak about his relationship with God.

I've been to visitations and funerals for the lost (those without hope for eternal life with Jesus) and for those who knew they were saved. There are many obvious differences, but the one I observed the most at this visitation was the blank stare on most everyone's faces. There wasn't much hope.

In tying these two subjects together (the movie about George Bailey and the young man that died), I started to ask *myself* a very different question; not *"What would life be life if I'd never been born?"* but *"What would life be like for others if I'd died when I was only 22 years old?"* I'll save the fact that three kids would never have been born and a thousand plus other people would have never known me or met me.

More specifically, what would my eternal destination have looked like had I died before I'd trusted Jesus Christ as my Lord and Savior? I'll tell you where I'd be—in hell. Not only would I be suffering physically, but I would be consciously aware of an eternal separation from God, knowing that I could do nothing to change that—ever! For eternity!

I hope that scares the hell out of you! And I hope you know what I mean by that (for more details on trusting Jesus Christ as your Lord and Savior, see the Appendix).

There's something else I consider about my life: all the people I've had the opportunity to minister to since I was 22 years old. The way that God has placed me in certain situations and with certain people still amaze me to this day. I've done nothing to earn His grace and mercy. I don't hold a special degree of favoritism with God. Often, I think back to Him speaking through me and putting words in my mouth and giving me recall for Scriptures to bless others. Do you think I've done something special to merit that? I hope I don't burst you bubble, but I have not.

In closing, I want to ask you a question. This life, the one you're living right now, is it a *wonderful life?* I don't mean everyone in town showing up at your front door and dumping enough money on your kitchen table to bail you out of jail, put your kids through college, and pay off your mortgage. Honestly, sometimes the way we look at like makes all the difference in the world. Our situations may remain the same, but our perspectives and views of those situations will change if we have the right heart-attitude (see Mark 8:36, Matthew 6:33).

Life can be amazing, or wonderful, if we let Jesus Christ have control. Read the verse below the title of this chapter again. It says, "You will show me the path of **life**..." Who will show you the path of life? God will. Then, and only then, no matter what happens, you will never look at life the same way.

Mom and Dad

In the fear of the LORD there is strong confidence,
and his children will have refuge.
Proverbs 14:26 (NASB)

Since you read in the dedication about when my father passed away, let me share a few things about him and my mom without going into too many details, and then give you a challenge.

Dad and Mom were living in a nursing home in California. Mom had gone there first after falling and breaking her hip, along with experiencing some other health issues. My parents were seldom apart from each other in their 66 years of marriage. All Dad could think about was getting up and getting ready each day to go see his "honey."

One night while I was in California visiting with Dad, I witnessed an episode of what would eventually be labeled early dementia. My two older brothers didn't believe me at first, until I let them listen to what I recorded on my phone.

It was just a matter of time before we had to make the decision for Dad's own safety to move him into the same facility as Mom. He had fallen a few times, but thankfully he was not seriously injured. Once again, his life revolved around Mom. Each morning, as soon as he was up, he would get ready and go to her room to spend the day with her.

Eventually, due to a vacancy, it became possible for them to be placed in same room. What a blessing for each of them that was!

The last time I saw Mom and Dad was the week of Christmas in 2012. Unlike the last half-dozen or so visits I'd made over the years (I live in Tennessee), this goodbye was different. A few months later, I knew why.

I called often and spoke with my brothers who lived nearby. My middle brother Tim lived closer than my oldest brother Daniel. Tim kept me more up-to-date with Mom and Dad because he was unemployed during the time they were in the nursing home. His new full-time job was seeing to many of the needs of our parents, talking with doctors, staying informed about their medications, and dealing with staff at the nursing home regarding their care.

Fast forward to Friday, March 29, 2013. As I had done for years, I would journal a prayer to the Lord after my morning quiet-time. The length of the prayer would depend on my thoughts, prayers, and the time available. On that day, I wrote the following words:

" *Lord, I never thought I would be able to have my father alive till this day, his 90th birthday. This last year has been very hard for him and Mom living in the nursing home, Dad getting worse in his mind, Mom with her health. However, through all this, you never stopped working in the lives of our family—meeting the emotional needs one by one; for me, You have brought me to the point of peace, knowing they will soon be with You. I don't know when that will be, but I trust You to carry all our hearts through the time of mourning – yet celebrating their home-going. Although I know it will be hard, I know I need to call Dad today. As I ponder in my heart and mind how I'll get through a call like that, I ask You Lord, give him as clear a mind and voice as he had over a year ago—just a glimpse to know who he is and to know me one last time. I love You Abba Father. Amen.*"

When I called Dad that day, he had a clear mind and voice, and he knew who he was and who I was! Between talking with him and my mom, we had talked for almost 10 minutes!

The next morning, I got up early to go running, and before I was about to leave, I noticed I had a voice message from my brother Tim. My heart melted inside as I listened to him say that the time of our Dad's home-going was at 11:44 PM, on his 90th birthday. The last time I spoke with him, God answered my prayers specifically. You know what else was special about that day? It was Good Friday. What better day than that to go meet Jesus face-to-face?

Later that day, as hard as it was to bring myself to say the words, I told Mom it was okay to go see Dad. She was so weak, so frail, so ready to go. Her heart was now broken in a way she'd never experienced before, and I knew she would not last long.

On Tuesday, four days later, I prayed a strange prayer., as I was on my treadmill at home from work. For years, I had asked God to keep my parents alive. I wasn't ready to let them go. That early evening about half-way through my run, I asked God to take Mom to her heavenly home. I still find this hard to describe, but I heard a voice, not audibly, but clearly, in my mind. "Eleanor, it's time to come home." Overwhelmed with tears, I managed to finish my run and make my way downstairs. I had another voice message from Tim. Mom has taken her last breath and had joined Dad in glory. When I realized what time she had passed—precisely at the time I'd heard the voice—I praised God through many tears of joy.

So here is my challenge. You can't out-ask God. Nothing is too small for God not to care about, and nothing is too big that God can't handle it. Does He answer prayers like He did for me every time? The way I prayed? No. But He answers nonetheless. We don't know the mind of God or the ways of God. He is sovereign (see Isaiah 55:8-9). However, He never said in His word, "Don't ask me anything, I already know what you need." On the contrary, Jesus said in Matthew 7:7-8, "Ask, and it will be given to you; seek, and you will find; knock, and it will be opened to you. For everyone who asks receives, and he who seeks finds, and to him who knocks it will be opened."

I can't explain it all, my friends, but I do know that God answers prayer. Sometimes specifically, sometimes using others, and in so many other ways. I love the way James 5:16 puts it: "Confess your trespasses to one another, and pray for one another, that you may be healed. The effective, fervent prayer of a righteous man avails much."

I have one last thing to share with you about my parents. It was during the time when Mom was in the nursing home and before Dad started living there. I was back at their house that night after spending time with them that day. Dad was still at the nursing home, always wanting to stay as late as he could. One of my brothers was planning to bring him home later. I was standing in their kitchen making dinner and listening to some music on my phone.

It always amazes me how God can use songs to touch our hearts and move us closer to Him in worship. He did it again that night. Chris Tomlin's version of *Everlasting God* was playing when a couple of lines made me stop and raise my hands in worship, and I began crying and pouring my heart out to the Lord. Now, every time I hear that song, I can't help but flash back to that night when I was worshipping and weeping to my God, all at the same time.

I suggest you look up the entire lyrics and listen to the song as soon as you can; which includes the words: ***You're the defender of the weak, You comfort those in need***.

Motorcycles and Snowplows

Because, although they knew God, they did not glorify *Him* as God,
nor were thankful, but became futile in their thoughts,
and their foolish hearts were darkened.
Romans 1:21

I admit that title above sounds rather crazy, but I'm confident before you're done reading this, you'll see how it fits together.

I received what I would call a compliment from one of the team members that went with me to Bogota, Colombia years back. It sticks with me till this day. It came as a surprise and something I wouldn't have thought of on my own. He said he likes the way I *think outside the box*. I've given that compliment some thought and have looked back on some of the things I've written over the years, and I guess I do tend to *think differently* on occasion. So, with that in mind, let me give you a scenario.

Fall is just one week away from the time I write this, and a promised frigid winter is just ahead (or so the experts say). With that in mind, there is always the possibility that we will have some snow around here. If we get any, it usually comes and goes in a couple days, so it's not that bad. If it doesn't snow here, I won't have to travel very far to find it.

I've ridden my motorcycle in some various weather conditions, but I have never intentionally or accidentally ridden it in the snow. Let's say we do get a very hard winter this year and that we have more than a few inches of snow. Then picture this next scene in your mind.

You look out the window one morning after a snow storm and see your neighbor trying to clear the snow off his driveway. That doesn't sound out of the ordinary, does it? Yet this neighbor is not using a shovel or conventional snowplow. What he's using is his motorcycle! You're dumbfounded as you watch him trying harder and harder, rolling it forward, revving the engine over and over, pushing the bike backwards, revving the engine again and again. All the while, the tires are slipping and sliding side to side. On and on he continues with no success. It is obvious to you he's not making any headway.

Now how foolish does this scenario seem to you, really? Unless it were a trike (a 3-wheeled motorcycle) equipped with snow chains and a plow in front, he won't win the battle. But this sort of thing happens every day all around us.

What I mean is that people are using something for a purpose for which it was never intended. Every manufacturer makes something for a purpose. They sometimes advise against its misuse and may even include warnings against using in a way that was never intended. Sort of like using a motorcycle as a snowplow. Ridiculous, isn't it?

Can you think of the number one thing that is misused today above all others? May I suggest it is not a *thing* at all but people themselves? God designed people for a purpose. But many people today are *using* themselves for a purpose that was never intended. They are abusing their bodies. They are abusing their minds. And they are running from God. They are not opening and following the very set of instructions that God wrote which explains clearly His purpose.

Normally at this point I would put a passage of Scripture in parentheses for you to look up. However, I really want to make sure you read this text and understand what God's word says about the *misuse* of something, in other words, as I mentioned, *people are using something for the purpose in which it was never intended to be used for.*

> [18] But God shows his anger from heaven against all sinful, wicked people who suppress the truth by their wickedness. [19] They know the truth about God because he has made it obvious to them. [20] For ever since the world was created, people have seen the earth and sky. Through everything God made, they can clearly see his invisible qualities—his eternal power and divine nature. So they have no excuse for not knowing God.

[21] Yes, they knew God, but they wouldn't worship him as God or even give him thanks. And they began to think up foolish ideas of what God was like. As a result, their minds became dark and confused. [22] Claiming to be wise, they instead became utter fools. [23] And instead of worshiping the glorious, ever-living God, they worshiped idols made to look like mere people and birds and animals and reptiles.

[24] So God abandoned them to do whatever shameful things their hearts desired. As a result, they did vile and degrading things with each other's bodies. [25] They traded the truth about God for a lie. So they worshiped and served the things God created instead of the Creator himself, who is worthy of eternal praise! Amen. [26] That is why God abandoned them to their shameful desires. Even the women turned against the natural way to have sex and instead indulged in sex with each other. [27] And the men, instead of having normal sexual relations with women, burned with lust for each other. Men did shameful things with other men, and as a result of this sin, they suffered within themselves the penalty they deserved.

[28] Since they thought it foolish to acknowledge God, he abandoned them to their foolish thinking and let them do things that should never be done. [29] Their lives became full of every kind of wickedness, sin, greed, hate, envy, murder, quarreling, deception, malicious behavior, and gossip. [30] They are backstabbers, haters of God, insolent, proud, and boastful. They invent new ways of sinning, and they disobey their parents. [31] They refuse to understand, break their promises, are heartless, and have no mercy. [32] They know God's justice requires that those who do these things deserve to die, yet they do them anyway. Worse yet, they encourage others to do them, too. (Romans 1:18-32; NLT)

So how do we lovingly approach such individuals? Notice I used the word *lovingly.* We don't judge, we don't criticize, we don't talk behind their backs and watch them misuse themselves, and we certainly don't seclude ourselves from them. We don't call their sin worse just because it looks different from our sin (ouch!). Yes, think about that for a minute. You know what Scripture that reminds me of? Luke 18:10-14. Go ahead and read it, but to summarize, the issue addressed there is *pride*. Whenever we think we're better than someone else or look down on somebody, it is pride showing off its ugly head of sin.

The way to love people and win them to Christ, is not to cast the first stone. People will know us by our love (read I John). If people knew we genuinely cared for them and loved them, and if they saw us loving each other as well, they would come in masses asking how they too can know our love of God. Through His forgiveness, we would then have numerous opportunities to show them God's purpose and plan for their lives and the purpose for which they were created.

My Bible

For the word of God is living and powerful, and sharper than any two-edged sword, piercing even to the division of soul and spirit, and of joints and marrow, and is a discerner of the thoughts and intents of the heart.
Hebrews 4:12

The year was 2005. The location, Hatfield, AR. The occasion, the Christian Motorcyclists Association (CMA) National Rally. It was also the year that I bought what would turn out to be my favorite Bible. The CMA headquarters is in Hatfield, AR West of Hot Springs.

During that same rally I heard the testimony of a man who smuggled Bibles into house churches in China. Since he was wanted by the Chinese government, he went by the name Joseph Lee while here in the States to protect his identity. I'll never forget one of the stories he told, as I sat there holding my new Bible.

He described the details of secretly meeting with a group of underground Christians as he was about to give them *a* Bible. That's right, he was giving *a group of believers, a Bible.* They were scarce in that region, and the pastor would be the one to care for it. He would also be the one to go to prison for life—or worse, be executed—if the authorities ever found out he had it.

Joseph Lee said he handed the Bible to the pastor, who then passed it to each person in the group, about 20 of them. Joseph was sitting next to the pastor in the small, dark, candle lit, cramped room, as the Bible was returned to him. As Joseph looked down at the Bible, now back in the pastor's hands, he saw that the cover was soaked with the tears of the believers.

God's written word was so precious to them, and to finally see it and touch it, *the whole bible at once,* made them weep over it with joy and thanksgiving as they held it close to their faces.

Fast forward thirteen years. That same Bible I bought at that rally has been nearly as precious to me as the one those Chinese believers had held for the first time. Many of my friends have seen that Bible and have asked about it. To me it is very precious. Much prayer, studying, weeping, lots of notes, and many memory verses later, you can imagine what that Bible meant to me.

Yes, *meant,* as in past tense. My wife and I had gone out to lunch one afternoon and discovered upon our return that our 10-month-old lab-mix puppy, Zoey, had got ahold of my Bible.

I had not left it on the floor or anywhere else we thought she could reach. I had left it sitting on the kitchen counter where it had been many times before. I didn't lose my temper with her. All I did was ask my wife to put her outside while I sat on the floor and stared at what remained of my Bible. Eventually I gathered the pieces and placed them in a small box. I didn't shed a tear over this loss, but I must admit I felt broken-hearted over it.

You may find it hard to believe—and if you had seen what Zoey had done to it, you might sympathize with the effort a little more—but I was able to painstakingly put together parts of the New Testament again, from Romans 1 to Revelation 3. The brown leather cover was completely consumed, including a special sticker in the front cover, that helped me remember my first mission trip ten years prior to Bogota, Colombia.

Is your Bible as precious to you as mine was? Do you have so many notes, underlined sections, worn pages, and maybe some tape holding it together in places that it's obvious you spend time in it? I don't ask that as if I'm bragging about what mine looked like. I ask it, because I know that's what God would want from you: to appreciate and love His word so much, that you would get the cover wet with your tears.

Ironically, the next week at church, our pastor talked about how many people in the United States have Bibles in their homes (on average 4.5 per household) and how many people read them 3-4 times per week (about 22% on average). In comparison to the house church in China, it's sad that we have so many Bibles sitting on our shelves and so little use for them.

Do you hunger and thirst for His righteousness and for His word daily? Is it your heart's desire to get to know God by spending time with Him in His word? I hope so. My favorite time of the day is first thing in the morning while I'm the only one up and it's still dark out. My routine is to lay everything out the night before, so after I'm up and I get my coffee, I'm ready to spend time in prayer, read a devotion, meditate on His word, be still and ready to spend time with my Lord and Savior Jesus Christ.

In closing I wanted to leave you with just a few of my favorite verses. I've put these and many more to memory, and I challenge you to do the same.

"But He answered and said, "It is written, 'Man shall not live by bread alone, but by every word that proceeds from the mouth of God" (Matthew 4:4).

"Therefore we also, since we are surrounded by so great a cloud of witnesses, let us lay aside every weight, and the sin which so easily ensnares us, and let us run with endurance the race that is set before us, 2 looking unto Jesus, the author and finisher of our faith, who for the joy that was set before Him endured the cross, despising the shame, and has sat down at the right hand of the throne of God" (Hebrews 12:1-2).

"Your word I have hidden in my heart, That I might not sin against You" (Psalm 119:11).

People, Places, Things

Then King David went in and sat before the LORD, and he said:
"Who am I, Sovereign LORD, and what is my family,
that you have brought me this far?
2 Samuel 7:18 (NIV)

As you begin to read this, I'd like you to think about your past. You may recall many happy memories, or you may have nothing but painful ones. But even if your memories are painful, let me ask you a question. Have you ever thought about the people that impacted you the most? Maybe it was a parent, a sibling, a neighbor, a coach, or perhaps someone you knew very little, but their actions or words impacted you for the rest of your life.

If your past was painful, do you think God cared? Or do you think He was too busy helping others to see your tears, hears your cries, or feel your pain. Maybe you believe God is limited in what He can and can't do. This won't be a consideration about the sovereignty of God, but I will say unapologetically, that I firmly believe in it. That, my friends, is a topic for discussion at another time.

What I want to share with you is how I have seen God's hand at work in my life, and then conclude with an observation.

People impact our lives for good and for bad. The places we've been and the experiences we've had all make an impact on us. Have you ever thought about if you were at a certain place at a certain time that the outcome of a situation would have turned out different? And what about the decisions we've made? Have you ever lived with regret? Have you ever wished you did or did not do something in your life? Do you think that God has used our own decisions to change us? Never forget this—God is sovereign—He uses our free will for His glory.

On more than one occasion, God has worked specifically in my life by using devotionals from Oswald Chambers[20] that have personally impacted my life. I believe He has done that because of specific things I have been going through and have been praying about. Things specific to do with my story! Hallelujah! God cares that much about each one of us! More about that at the end.

One of my favorite stories in the Old Testament is the life of Joseph. Obviously, we see from cover to cover, the whole story. But can you imagine having lived that story? God sees our cover-to-cover story. He doesn't wonder how it's going to turn out. He knows. We know how Joseph's life turned out, all for the good of the people of Israel, right? Joseph, even after all he went through, after it was over, saw that what his brothers did to him was used by God to accomplish His plans.

We see Joseph's conclusion with his epiphany in *Genesis 50:20.* "You intended to harm me, but God intended it for good to accomplish what is now being done, the saving of many he experiences we've had lives."

But what about our lives? Don't you wish at times we could see from one end to the other, all the people, places, and things that have happened and how they will all work out? But, on second thought, would we really want to see the result before it takes place? I wouldn't. I can tell you right now, by knowing what would happen, even if like Joseph's life, we'd avoid the pain and try to get to the end before we've been proven or tested.

I'm thankful for the pain—on this end looking back, that is. Will there be more? I'm sure there will be. All of us have pain, trials, tests, temptations. The key is *fixing our eyes on Jesus* (see Hebrews 12:2). He will strengthen us, He will comfort us, and remember, there is purpose in the pain.

---

[20] *Wikipedia, The Free Encyclopedia*, s.v. "Oswald Chambers," (accessed December 8, 2018), https://en.wikipedia.org/wiki/Oswald_Chambers

As I'd mentioned, I had my own epiphany recently. It took place on a Friday, the 13th. By the way, there is nothing *superstitious* about that day either. I flat out disbelieve the myths and am convinced it's just another tool Satan uses to take our minds off God.

I'd made a personal commitment to myself about 6 months prior, and here it was, Friday the 13th, with 13 days left before the fulfillment of that commitment. I had to smile. The Lord knows what dates mean to me and how He's used them in my life to show me certain things.

In fact, it was on April 13th one year that I surrendered my heart to Him once again. He was tugging at my heart and overwhelming me with His presence that day.

I'd mentioned the Oswald Chambers devotion and will conclude with the impact it made on me because I too felt like I wandered in the desert until God called my name.

The devotion that day mentioned Moses after he was grown, when he went out to his brethren and looked at their burdens (Exodus 2:11). He saw the oppression of his people and thought he was the one to save them. After his anger led him to murder an Egyptian, and as he was found out, he fled into the desert to feed sheep for forty years.

Finally, God appeared to him and said, "...bring My people...out of Egypt. But Moses said to God, 'Who am I that I should go...?" (see Exodus 3:10-11). After 40 years of training, he was finally a changed person, after he had learned true fellowship and oneness with God.

I must admit that I've felt like Moses at times in the past. I thought I was doing what God wanted me to do, yet it must have been me. I know now I wasn't ready then.

Oswald's devotion on the 13th says, "We must also learn that our *individual effort* (emphasis mine) for God shows nothing but disrespect for Him— our individuality is to be rendered radiant through a personal relationship with God, so that He may be "well pleased" (Matthew 3:17).

119

It took Moses 40 years before he was ready spiritually for God to use him to take the children of Israel out of Egypt and begin the journey into the Promised Land. Unfortunately, it took the people another 40 years to arrive. The title of this book, *From Wilderness to Worship, A 40 Day Journey,* speaks volumes of my journey. One day, I'll have more to say about that journey.

In closing, is God giving you a hunger for fellowship with Him the more you seek Him? Do you feel that the more you worship Him, the more you desire to be humbled and used by Him? All we need to ask the Lord is that He would bring Glory and Honor to His Name alone, no matter what is takes. After all, isn't that true surrender?

Potholes

Where there is no guidance the people fall
Proverbs 11:14a (NASB)

I used to drive an older car that was nearing 300,000 miles on it before I finally gave it away (now I hear it has over 300,000 and still running).

One of the key ingredients I believe that kept the car going so long was performing regular maintenance and treating it with a whole lot of TLC, especially as it got older and more miles on it. One of the many ways I gave it some practical TLC was avoiding–at almost any cost– the possibility of hitting any potholes wherever I drove. That's not an easy task where I live!

If for some reason I did happen to be taken by surprise and hit one of those potholes unexpectedly, I would grit my teeth and let out an audible, "Ugh!" and hope for the best that the "Ole Green Machine" would come out on the other side of the pothole unscathed.

I don't think anyone, regardless of the kind of vehicle they drive, enjoys going through a pothole on the road.

Now that I drive a newer car, I want to avoid those potholes for another reason: I don't want to cause any damage to it.

One of these potholes I must avoid is just down the street from my work. It didn't start out as a pothole though. It began as some loose blacktop just towards the outside right portion of the lane, near the gravel and the grass. It was hardly noticeable.

However, every time a car drove over that area, slowly, and over the course of time, it began to ebb away. Since a minor repair was never taken care in the first place, this small loose black top has now become a deep, dangerous, wide, pothole in the entire right side of the lane!

If it remains unattended much longer, it will require a lane closure and some major repair work to fix it.

We've all seen holes like this in the areas where we live. A feeble attempt to repair them by pouring some gravel in it and packing it down rarely, if ever, fixes the problem. Or maybe someone tries putting in a couple shovel loads of some hot asphalt and packing it down. To me that is simply trying to put a Band-Aid on a bullet wound.

I'm no pavement expert by any means, but I'll bet the best way to fix a pothole is to cut further around the original damaged hole and fill it in properly with the right mixture, and then pack it tight and smooth it out flat so it looks as close to the original road as possible.

A better solution would be to make repairs before a major fix is necessary by paying close attention to potential holes and taking care of them before major damage is done.

We don't refer to them as "potholes" when our lives need repair or are in need of major overhauling. But we may call them other things. They could be wounds from the past (emotional or physical), unforgiveness toward someone, betrayal from a close friend or relative, a season of depression that seems to worsen as times passes, anger at someone or some situation, bitterness, jealousy, hatred, or myriad other possibilities. There are a lot of words we could use to describe those "potholes" in our lives.

Any of these things, if left unrepaired, will just get worse and worse until major construction is necessary. I once heard a pastor tell about cases of actual physical illnesses that could be directly related to and pinpointed back to the emotional scars that took place in a person's life.

More often than we care to admit, one of the temporary "fixes" we attempt in trying to repair our own lives is to find people we can talk to about them. I once read a question that personally convicted me, and I had to ask it of myself. The question was, "Do you pray about it as much as you talk about it?" Human nature is to want to talk about our problems or seek counsel when we're faced with heavy loads in our lives. That is not entirely wrong. According to Proverbs 11:4, it's wise to do this: "Where there is no guidance the people fall, but in abundance of counselors there is victory" (NASB).

In the most hopeless situations is where people have thrown in the towel and given up. But God is the very One who has asked us to give Him our burdens (see Matthew 11:28). He is the One who wants to hear from you. He is the One to talk to about what hurts and give to Him those things that cause pain, so He can do the healing, not ten mutual friends. I'm not saying we shouldn't talk to others at all about these things, but I am saying we need to pay close attention to what God's word says (see James 1:19-20).

We also tend to find people that will agree with us or that can see our side of the story when it comes to ill feelings toward another person or when we're trying to justify our actions in a situation. In doing that we're attempting to elevate ourselves (pride of self over others).

Trust me on this. I've been there, done that, and "got the t-shirt" as the old saying goes. What about you? As you have read this, did some old situations and people from your past come to your mind? Can you think of the last time you did what was described?

What we end up doing when we take that route is temporarily fixing the potholes I've mentioned. Putting a little gravel in the hole and packing it down may even satisfy us for a short time. The reality is that although it may fix it temporarily, the "wound" is never correctly addressed.

Let's look at Gods word and a few lives that were affected by their own potholes in life.

King David had some potholes that had gone unrepaired long before his adulterous affair with Bathsheba and the murder of Bathsheba's husband Uriah. If his "road" had been smooth and free of potholes or loose gravel, he would have quickly turned aside to "flee from sin" rather than run to it like he did when he and saw her bathing. Dr. Adrian Rogers, my former pastor, used to quote Oswald Chambers when teaching about King David, "An unguarded strength is a double weakness." [21]

King Solomon in all his wisdom had a few potholes, too—about 700 plus 300 of them to be close (see 1 Kings 11:1-13). His potholes caused him a great deal of damage. They turned his heart away from worshipping the One True God.

We may not be able to avoid the potholes on the road every time, nor may we be able to avoid the occasional "potholes" that occur in our lives, but there are just a few practical steps we can take to repair the small ones before they get too big. Even if you do need major work in your life, and if it seems overwhelming right now, take heart. There is hope.

1. Start praying about it. Don't talk to about it with anyone else, but really take it before the Lord. Talk to Him as if you were sharing your heart with a friend. He *is* a friend. Take it to Him often until you feel as if He has given you some peace in your heart about it.

2. Read Scripture. There's nothing—and I mean absolutely nothing—that will heal wounds better than God's word (see Psalm 30:2, 103:2-4, 119:11, 147:3).

3. Have faith. Oh, how easy that sounds and so hard to believe, right? But GOD! There's those two words again. It is true, and

---

[21] "Oswald Chambers quote:," azquotes.com/quote/927847 (accessed December 8, 2018).

they really do mean that when all seems to fall in around us, when the waves are crashing over our heads, He steps in and takes control. After praying, after meditating on His word, believe in His promises that only HE can bring healing to your potholes. Then, and only then, can you start to see the smooth road again.

Reasons to Believe the Bible

For the word of God is living and powerful, and sharper than any two-edged sword, piercing even to the division of soul and spirit, and of joints and marrow, and is a discerner of the thoughts and intents of the heart.
Hebrews 4:12

I remember playing chess one time with a friend. He was someone I'd had many discussions with about the validity of Scripture and that Jesus was who He said He was. Each time we talked, he would tell me he didn't believe what I said was true. That was fine for me, but not for him, and he expressed that he basically believed in relativism.[22]

He excused himself for a minute to use the restroom while we were playing. Once again, I was a little frustrated trying to share my beliefs with him, and I was trying to find a way to show him that the word of God was true, while at the same time showing him that what he believed could never be true. I had an idea. Before he came back, I took the chess pieces and exchanged his queen for mine, his rook for mine, his bishop for mine, and a few pawns (we were using the traditional black and white pieces).

When he returned, he immediately started complaining that I had messed up the game and argued that we couldn't play chess with the colors of the pieces mixed up. I told him I thought we could and took his relativism argument a step further. I said, *"What's right for you may be all the colors on one side, but I think they can be mixed."* He grew a little more upset and blurted out, *"You can't play that way. It's against the rules!"* I said, *"Against the what?"* He exclaimed, *"The rules!"*

I looked at him with genuine sincerity and replied, *"And the same goes for life my friend. We can't just believe that what is right for you*

---

[22] *Wikipedia, The Free Encyclopedia*, s.v. "Relativism," (accessed December 8, 2018), https://en.wikipedia.org/wiki/Relativism

may not be right for me. There must be absolute truth! It's against God's rules to believe otherwise. That's why He gave us His rule book."

What about you? Have you ever shared the message of salvation with someone, only to feel immediate resistance and arguments about the validity of Scripture? Then you're not alone. I call them *smoke screens,* because I believe the bottom line is that they're avoiding admitting their sin, even though they won't call it that nor acknowledge that they are avoiding it.

Remember, our job is simply to share Christ and the message of salvation with others, not to convert them by our own wisdom. I've heard it said that if you convince a man to come to Christ, you'll have to continually convince him to stay there. Objections may not always be bad, but some people just seem to have hard hearts.

I want to give you four reasons to believe the Bible is true, because it is the very Word of God. I must give credit to the late pastor Adrian Rogers[23] for these reasons. I didn't write them, but I do share them with people across the country every week.

The first reason is the **Scientific Accuracy of the Bible**. When the facts of science are ultimately revealed they always support the Bible. The Bible tells us of a round earth in Isaiah 40:22, hanging in space in Job 26:7, in the middle of countless galaxies and stars in Jeremiah 33:22, hundreds of years before scientists admitted the same. Scientists don't discover anything that God hasn't already created.

The second reason is the **Historical Accuracy of the Bible**. Numerous archeologists and geologists have set out to disprove the Bible's historical accuracy. Each time they have tried, they have

---

[23] Love Worth Finding Ministries *with Adrian Rogers,* lwf.org/questions-and-answers/what-evidence-is-there-that-the-bible-is-in-fact-gods-word (accessed December 8, 2018).

discovered greater evidence that supports the Bible. Even secular history records numerous accounts that go along with the record of the Bible.

The third reason is the **Unity of the Bible**. The Bible Is made up of 66 different books. It was written by at least 40 different authors over a period of 1600 years in about 13 different countries and in three languages. Despite all that, the Bible reads as if it were one book. It is constantly reaffirming itself, always with the message of salvation through faith in Jesus Christ and no one else.

The fourth reason is the **Fulfilled Prophecy of the Bible**. Regarding Jesus alone, there are more than 300 Old Testament prophesies that are fulfilled by Him in the New Testament.

Let's expand the idea of the fulfilled prophecy of Jesus a little just so you can try to wrap your mind around the possibility that He really is the One written about in the Old Testament.

Imagine that there are millions and millions of coins stacked 2 feet high across the entire state of Texas. One of those coins is marked red. That one coin is hidden somewhere amongst the other coins.

Imagine now an airplane flying somewhere over the state, and inside the plane a man with a parachute. Just before he jumps, he is blindfolded. When he safely lands somewhere on the pile of coins, somewhere in Texas, he reaches down and pulls up the coin marked red. What do you think the chances are of that happening?

There is a better chance of someone doing that than Jesus Christ fulfilling only seven of those 300 prophesies about Himself. Yet He fulfilled every one of them.

Do you or someone you know need more proof that Jesus Christ existed? I suggest you do a little research in secular history records.[24]

---

[24] *Wikipedia, The Free Encyclopedia*, s.v. "Historicity of Jesus," (accessed December 8, 2018), https://en.wikipedia.org/wiki/Historicity_of_Jesus

Most of Jesus' disciples were martyred for their belief in Him too. There may be some men that are willing to live for a lie, but not many would die for a lie.

I would also suggest doing some research on your own into the legitimacy of Scripture by looking at the life of award-winning journalist Lee Strobel and the account of his journey from atheism to faith.[25]

I told you that there are four reasons to believe the Bible. There is one more. It is me. You can argue all you want with me face-to-face about what *you* believe is the truth, but I know Jesus Christ as my personal Lord and Savior. I believe with all my heart that the Bible is the Word of God. The Bible says that Jesus answers prayer. I have personally experienced that in my life. If I didn't believe those things, my life would be a train wreck, because that's where I was headed. Jesus Christ changed my life, and He can change your life too!

Jesus said in John 14:6, "I am the way, the truth, and the life. No one can come to the Father except through Me." Jesus is the Messiah.

I will close by asking for a response from you. The Bible says in Luke 19:10, "for the Son of Man [Jesus] has come to seek and to save that which was lost." The *which* is us.

While you've been reading this, one of three things has happened. First, you might have agreed with everything you've read, because you already know Jesus Christ personally. If so, praise the Lord!

Or you may have made up your mind to remain cold in your heart and to resist the Holy Spirit of God. You deny that the Bible is the very Word of God. Your sin is that are still denying that Jesus Christ can be your Lord and Savior.

Or maybe, while you have been reading, the Holy Spirit has been putting His gentle finger on your heart and convicting you, and He has been drawing you closer to Him.

---

[25] Lee Strobel, "About Lee," leestrobel.com/about/ (accessed December 9, 2018).

If are you ready to come to Him and lay down your burdens and confess your sin of living for self, and give your life to Him, may I suggest you stop and just pray and tell God what you're feeling and ask Him to reveal Himself to you. The Holy Spirit will pinpoint what needs to be confessed just by pouring your heart out.

Romans 10:9-10 says, "that if you confess with your mouth the Lord Jesus and believe in your heart that God has raised Him from the dead, you will be saved. For with the heart one believes unto righteousness, and with the mouth confession is made unto salvation."

Relationships

Do nothing out of selfish ambition or vain conceit. Rather,
in humility value others above yourselves, not looking to your
own interests but each of you to the interests of the others.
Philippians 2:3 (NIV)

I started writing this chapter when I was on vacation one year, visiting family in California. Before I go any further, read that first sentence again and see if there's a word in it that brings up memories while you were growing up, whether good or bad. Do you see it? I hope you did. It's the word *family.*

I still have two older brothers that live in California, one who is married with kids and grandkids, and one who is single. I'm not going to bore you to death with details, although I could tell you some hilarious stories, some of which took place while there. What I will say about it, though, is that *family* can be messy. Would you agree? It can also be the best thing that has ever happened, so I count it a blessing!

I started thinking about the real meaning of *relationships*, and some things that happened around another vacation time I had. Funny thing is, I do a lot of *thinking* about life when my mind isn't consumed with work. I don't disengage my mind. Rather I have deeper, more far-reaching thoughts about life.

Let me tell you about some of the relationships I have in life. I fact, what I'm about to share with you came from a journal entry I wrote one morning. This all took place within a few days, and it showed me what the Lord can do if we're just willing to let Him direct our paths.

Hannah and Brian, two of our grandkids, are unique in their own ways. I love spending time with them every chance I get. One night, when they were spending the night at our house, our plan was to get up and go out to breakfast the next morning. But, when morning arrived, Hannah didn't want to get up. No matter how hard we tried, she wasn't budging.

Brian on the other hand, woke right up and was ready to go at the drop of a hat. They're different. And guess what? That's okay. I still have a relationship with them. They each get the part of me they need.

I remember visiting a friend of mine who is a member of a secular Motorcycle Club. It was completely out of my comfort zone to go see him. But I knew it was the Lord who prompted me to do so. Once the awkwardness wore off, I had a great time just sitting with him, hearing him share his heart and his *story* with me. I felt the Lord leading me as I shared things about my life with him and what all was on my heart. I also invited him to church and just felt the Lord leading me all the way. I prayed for him before I left and pray for a continued friendship to build there.

That same day I went to go see a friend of a friend I'd never met before. He was a veteran, and a former fire fighter, but now he was fighting for his life. I had no idea his exact condition, how he'd receive me, how long I'd stay or even what I'd say when I got there. His wife was there too, and it wasn't long before all three of us were sharing what God has done in our lives. He was very encouraged by my visit. Before I left, I prayed for their daughter, as they shared about her depression and suicidal thoughts. The Lord directed that prayer completely.

The next day I was on my way to Arkansas, to support and comfort some friends I've known for years. Unfortunately, it was at a visitation. Nobody I know wants to go through the loss of a parent, especially when it's by suicide, and especially on Christmas. There are no words that can be appropriately said at a time like that, only a hug, and just being there.

Personally, I cannot fathom the reason anyone would feel they needed to take his or her own life, nor can I image the pain the family was having. All I knew, is that the Lord asked us to comfort those that are hurting when they need us (see 2 Corinthians 1:3-4).

The following day I went to a funeral for a very precious lady. She was a wife, mother, grandmother and even a great grandmother. I had the privilege of knowing this woman, who was a saint in the eyes of many. I feel blessed to be able to say that, as well as knowing most of her family. I know the pain they were feeling first hand. They rejoiced in knowing her pain and suffering was over, and that she is now celebrating in Glory. Yet, the earthly pain we feel when we lose a loved one is real. God gave us these emotions, He created us with them.

The Holy Spirit spoke to my heart through each of those situations, as He does often. He revealed to me how it is only through obedience that we can be the hands and feet of Jesus towards others. He can do such incredible things!

I want to encourage you to follow God's heart. What do I mean by that? Ask yourself this question. What is on God's heart? People. "Do nothing out of selfish ambition or vain conceit. Rather, in humility value others above yourselves, not looking to your own interests but each of you to the interests of the others" (Philippians 2:3-4; NIV).

Trying to surrender wholeheartedly by partial surrender, is no surrender at all. You can't serve God and self at the same time. By self, I mean our own foolish pride. We don't come first. He does (see Matthew 23:12).

Satan The Thief

The thief does not come except to steal, and to kill,
and to destroy. I have come that they may have life,
and that they may have *it* more abundantly.
John 10:10

Fasten your seatbelts for my opening statement, but please don't take it personally: *What you believe or don't believe has absolutely no bearing on truth. Truth is truth; absolutely.*

Several years ago, a new production manager had been hired at my workplace, and we were getting to know one another. Through the course of his first week there, he made no apologies about the fact that he was an atheist. In fact, his beliefs came across even stronger when he found out I was a Christian.

Then it happened. Our discussion about what he *really believed was truth* was revealed. Let me remind you that truth is truth. What I mean is that just because you believe something to be true doesn't make it so. You may believe with all your heart that you could step off the roof of a 20-story building into thin air and not fall. But the truth is that gravity exists, and you'll fall to your death. You may believe you could walk on water like Peter did. Go ahead and try it. You'll find out just how fast you can sink.

So back to the manager. He gave me all the reasons why he didn't believe in God. Then I asked him this question: Do you think you know everything about everything? He gave me a puzzled look, so I repeated my question. Then I explained it further. I said, "Since it's impossible for any human being to know everything about everything, (which he finally admitted), would you then agree that it's possible that God exists beyond what *you personally* believe to be true?" He admitted it. So, he went from being an atheist to an agnostic[26].

Brothers and sisters, we are not called to *make* others believe what we believe. We are called to *share* what Jesus Christ has done in us, that's all. If our lives are absolutely surrendered to follow Him, then when we are sharing the message of the hope that lies within us (see 1 Peter 3:15), we are allowing the Holy Spirit to use our testimony to be a *fragrance* (see 2 Corinthians 2:14-17) for the gospel.

So, let me ask you a question. Where are you with Christ? Are you redeemed? Have you accepted that Jesus is exactly who He says He is? Only you can answer that for yourself. But, be careful. If you say that you are a Christian and that you have surrendered your life to Christ, and if you say He is Lord of your life, what does your life look like? Are you trying to see how far you can push the envelope without actually sinning? If you are, it may be that you're fooling yourself, and Satan has already *robbed you.*

The verse for this chapter is John 10:10, but I think verses 7-9 hold the key: "Then Jesus said to them again, 'Most assuredly, I say to you, I am the door of the sheep. All who *ever* came before Me are thieves and robbers, but the sheep did not hear them. I am the door. If anyone enters by Me, he will be saved, and will go in and out and find pasture.'"

In fact, if you go back to the beginning of chapter 10, verse 1 says, "Most assuredly, I say to you, he who does not enter the sheepfold by the door, but climbs up some other way, the same is a **thief and a robber**" (emphasis mine). Entering the sheepfold by The Door, Jesus Christ, is THE Way and THE Truth!

What does a thief typically do when he breaks into a home or business? He goes through the window, the back door, the garage, almost any other way than the front door. He certainly doesn't stand at

---

[26] *Wikipedia, The Free Encyclopedia*, s.v. "Agnosticism," (accessed, December 12, 2018), https://en.wikipedia.org/wiki/Agnosticism

the door, ring the bell, and wait for the homeowner to answer to then say, "Excuse me, may I come in and steal your valuables?"

One night early in our marriage, my wife and I went out to our favorite Chinese restaurant. Afterwards we picked up our son from my parent's and returned home. As we unlocked and opened the front door, we saw that the back door was wide open. It didn't take us long to look around the room and realize we had been robbed. A thief came in to steal. He destroyed our lives (temporarily), and he may even have harmed us if we had been at home.

There is another place the thief comes in that is not as obvious. He still climbs over the wall, but we don't see that. He says the right things, he sings the right songs, he may even join the rest, but he's a thief. He's a wolf in sheep's clothing. He's crept into your church and he's acted like he's become a part of the sheepfold. So how do you identify him? If you wait long enough, his true self will usually become known.

The Shepherd knows His sheep, but He may allow certain true sheep in His fold to be tested by the thief. Leave two of them alone long enough (the real sheep and the wolf dressed as a sheep), and before long, the wolf starts to hunger for that sheep. He begins by subtly casting doubt in the sheep's mind about the Shepherd, doubts about whether what He says is true. He will offer subtle lies, all the while hoping he can draw some away and devour them. Remember, friends, although the enemy will use people to attack us, "we do not wrestle against flesh and blood, but against principalities, against powers, against the rulers of the darkness of this age, against spiritual hosts of wickedness in the heavenly places" (Ephesians 6:12).

If you believe in The Truth (Jesus Christ) and that He is The Way (not one of many ways), that He will not lie, that what He said in His word will not return void (see Isaiah 55:11), and if you have confessed with your mouth that Jesus is Lord, and you believe in your heart that God raised Him from the dead (see Romans 10:9-10), you *will* be saved! Not maybe, not hopefully, but you will. Not because you keep doing good, because you can't *be* good. All you can do is abide in Him.

We could unpack ten different sermons or books in that last paragraph. Trust me, they've been preached, and they've been written. All I want you to see is this as we wrap up the subject on Satan the thief.

What made the difference in the lives of the disciples before Jesus' death, and after He died, rose from the dead, and ascended into heaven? The difference can be found in John 14:16-17. The disciples were filled with the Holy Spirit after Jesus ascended. He is the Spirit of Truth. He unveils Himself to those that come to Him. We don't get parts of Jesus as we grow in Christ; we get ALL of Him.

Jesus spent his time ministering to the masses but investing in twelve men. He even invested His life in one that would betray Him. They knew Him better than anyone else on Earth. The difference before the cross, was they all abandoned Him when He was arrested (see Matthew 26:56). But after His resurrection and ascension, they had a Holy Spirit boldness within them. Even though many were arrested and beaten, they still proclaimed His name.

It cost them their lives—brutal, horrible deaths. All they had to do was deny Jesus to spare their lives. They were willing to give their lives rather than deny who Jesus is. There are many that would be willing to live for a lie, but not many that would be willing to die for that lie.

Have you made the decision that Jesus is exactly who He said He is? He came here to pay the price for our sins. I don't care who you are, what you have done, how much money you have—there is nothing you can do to ever be good enough to stand before the God of the universe. There is only one way to stand before God and hear Him say *"Welcome home."* It is through Jesus. He said, "I am the way, the truth, and the life and no one comes to the Father except through Me" (John 14:6).

Signs

I set my rainbow in the cloud...
the **sign** of the covenant between Me and the earth.
Genesis 9:13 (Emphasis mine)

Have you ever thought much about signs? You know, road signs, instructional signs in buildings, airports, schools, the workplace, stores (not the advertisement ones), parks, police stations, etc.? They're all over the place. I don't think we give a second thought to most of them. Unless that sign is time sensitive, i.e. which gate your next flight departs from, or the unfamiliar city you're in when you suddenly come to the point of decision to take the highway going East or West. I've been in those situations more than I care to admit, and panic is usually what takes place.

There's a lot of positive results that come out of paying attention to signs. One I can think of is obeying the speed limit. The results? You don't get a ticket and pay a fine or court costs, you don't lose work because of said violation, you save money on your car insurance (no commercial advertisement intended), and you save yourself a lot of headaches by not speeding.

What else is a benefit of paying attention to signs? The speed limit sign isn't the only traffic law you can violate. Obeying other signs prevents that *not so friendly encounter* with Mr. Officer. Like the ones we obey for our own safety. Like the speed bumps sign. Have you ever ignored one of those? You know, the one that'll jar every bone in your body and make you wonder if you just left a few car parts behind you're about to observe in the rear-view mirror?

The signs I especially pay close attention to are the intersection stop signs and the traffic lights. Why? Because it seems where I live, people try run through them every chance they get. I've seen so many intersection crashes where the result of being in a hurry has even proven to be fatal.

Here are a few more signs I think you'll agree that when you obey them, you prevent accidents or even worse. Yield, caution, slow down, lane ends, dangerous curve, uneven lanes ahead, construction zone, no U-turn, one way, right turn only, and school zone.

The last one I'll mention is the one we used to see in California quite often. Especially when traveling near mountains and dense forests. We would tell our kids when they were younger, that there were *jumping deer* ahead!

Finally, and with less details, I even thought about some other types of signs we pay careful attention too or would be in our best interest to anyway. The gas gauge on our car is a *sign,* the monitor when you check your blood pressure is a *sign,* even when you step on the scale and see you might be eating a little too much is a *sign.*

You know what ALL those signs have in common? They are all man-made signs. Every size, shape, color, and meaning; man-made. And we pay attention and obey those man-made signs for what for our own personal safety or preservation.

Transition, application, explanation time, ready?

If (and I must assume at this point, since were not having a conversation) you obey and pay attention to most if not all those man-made signs, why then, for those of you that believe in the essentials, would you doubt, question, or disobey God? Do you believe the major things the bible teaches? That God is who He is, biblical creation, Jesus and the Virgin birth, the cross, the resurrection, heaven, and hell, just to mention a few things? If you believe those things because the bible teaches those subjects, then why would you ever have doubt or lack of faith in our all sovereign, loving, eternal God?

I mentioned faith in another chapter, but I'll remind you about it again as I illustrate this for you. How many times have you driven on a 2-

lane highway, be it at 35 miles per hour or 55 miles per hour, where the oncoming cars are passing you at equal or higher speeds, and at times within a few inches from your car? Multiple times would be my guess.

How much faith are you exercising in situations like that? How about the man-made bridge that goes across an expanse of water where if it would fail, you'd surely drown if it collapsed? Or how about the very means by which you were just in each of those situations, inside a vehicle put together by machines that were put together by men?

The sovereign Lord God, creator of all things seen, loves you so much, that He gave His Son Jesus Christ, as the perfect, sinless sacrifice, to once and for all, pay the penalty for sin. Too often, I've found myself putting more faith in my own abilities or in other people and things, than the God who created me.

I believe it would be wise for each of us to "Do your best to present yourself to God as one approved, a worker who does not need to be ashamed and who correctly handles the word of truth" (2 Timothy 2:15). By studying, and seeking the truth, God will reveal Himself more and more through the work of the Holy Spirit. You'll become more *spiritually fit* as you *exercise* your faith and believe Him for the signs He's given you in His word.

I'll close with a challenge. Make sure you read the chapter *Reasons to Believe the Bible.* But don't stop there. Take any doubts you have, to God. He has provided many signs in His word to follow. Jesus said in John 14:15-17, "If you love Me, keep My commandments. And I will pray the Father, and He will give you another Helper, that He may abide with you forever— the Spirit of truth, whom the world cannot receive, because it neither sees Him nor knows Him; but you know Him, for He dwells with you and will be in you."

Sports

Similarly, anyone who competes as an athlete does not receive
the victor's crown except by competing according to the rules.
2 Timothy 2:5 (NIV)

Junior High was not exactly what you would call *fun and interesting* for me. The fact is, only 2 months into Junior High we moved from IL where I'd gone to school since kindergarten, all the way to CA. I'd experienced the loss of everything familiar; friends, family, school, you name it. I celebrated my 12th birthday in a hotel room before we found a house to live in.

My physical appearance changed too. In IL I was not heavy at all. By the time I got started back in school I must have gained 30 pounds. I was the *new kid* that didn't fit right in with the crowd. I was behind in school. I wasn't athletic. I was picked on and made fun of almost from day one.

This was a Christian school, a very small one. So small, that when we played sports against rival schools, you were expected to play; may as well have been mandatory. And what did we do during PE? We played the sports through the seasons. Basketball, baseball, football. I had problems with every one of those sports. When you get picked last on the team, and you don't like playing, you're not very good. A vicious cycle.

My guess is, there may be a few of you reading this that can relate to me. It's almost as if it has left scars that have never quite healed. Memories of things are coming to my mind even now as I write. However bad some of those memories may be, there's a good one I want to share with you about sports.

It was time to practice baseball during PE class and somehow, I was the first baseman. I didn't usually play there, I much preferred the outfield, not as much of a chance messing up out there.

Remember I said I was picked on? Would you believe I had a personal *bully* that found it quite entertaining to go out of his way to make my life miserable? I think he was the one with problems, always had to prove himself as the best. He was held back at least one year, towered over most of the kids, and had biceps that you would see on High School athletes.

Back to first base. Guess who was at bat while I was playing first base? Yup, Mr. Bully. He gave me an evil grin as he got up to bat, almost as if he was warning me to stay clear when he ran by, or he wouldn't let me forget it. All he got was a base hit. The next guy got up. The bully takes a few steps off first, the pitcher looks over his shoulder, and decides he's stretching it a little too far and throws the ball at me to tag him.

Really? You think I want my lights punched out after school for tagging this guy out? No way Jose! So, I throw the ball back to the pitcher after Mr. Bully had jumped back to first. Pitcher is ready, looks, sees another lead off he thinks is too far, figures he can get him now, throws it hard, I catch it, swing down, safe. Now what on earth possessed me to do this next move is still beyond what you'd ever expect. I even shocked myself.

While Mr. Bully was looking away, dusting himself off from the slide back to first, I *acted* as if I threw the ball back to the pitcher, and the pitcher played along acting as if he caught it. Mr. Bully, not realizing the ball is hidden in my glove, looks at the pitcher winding up, takes his lead off and...you better believe I did! And you should have seen the look on his face when I tagged him out! It was priceless!

I thought for sure I was history after that, but believe it or not, he didn't knock my lights out after school, and didn't even pick on me as much after that.

A lot has changed since those days of playing sports, and even how involved parents are in their kid's sports activities today. All four of our kids played in some type of sports at some point growing up, and to be honest with you, even though we had some ruffled feathers at some of the calls made we believe were wrong, I never screamed or yelled or was asked to leave while my kids played. But some other parents? They acted like they bet money on their kids!

What about college and professional sports? Not the ones you or any of your kids play, what about the ones we pay to go see or the ones we watch on TV? Have you ever *lost it* while watching a game? You know what I mean. Or, on the opposite of the spectrum, have you ever been so excited your team was winning and beating the other team you were doing a happy dance in your living room?

Have you ever been that excited in church when a person is saved, baptized, or when the preacher makes a solid biblical point and asks for an Amen? I doubt it. I haven't.

Here's another thought regarding sports. Are we guilty of sitting around in our holy huddles discussing the game-plan in depth, so much so that we never actually get engaged in the game that God has placed us in for His purpose? I mean, we need to pray about it first, right? We must get clarification from the Lord before doing *anything* outside of our comfort zone, right?

A pastor I used to know would answer with a deep spiritual word at those arguments, it's called *Bologna*.

Do we think that the disciples stayed in their comfort zones and talked about the game-plan much? No, Jesus said it, they obeyed it! (most of the time). I wonder why Jesus sent out his disciples two by two? I think it was, so they wouldn't get comfortable sitting around with Jesus in His holy huddles.

Jesus said, "take up your cross and follow me" (see Matthew 16:24). The cross he referred to, was an instrument of death, it was not a nagging mother in law or a grumpy boss. Comfortable Christianity and couch potato Christians are toying with carnal Christianity when they take lightly the commands in His word and come up with a list of excuses.

147

A tree that bears no fruit shall be cut down and thrown into the fire (see Matthew 7:19).

As Christians today, we must be cautious to call what is unholy, holy, just so we can justify our actions. A lot of Churches have what they call *outreach* programs, designed to reach the lost. A lot of them are good, so please don't misunderstand me. They try to *draw the crowd to come and see*, when maybe our focus should be geared more towards *going to where the crowd is.* Or, maybe just to where some individuals are that need Jesus. Didn't Jesus model that for us?

Every year American's are consumed with the Super Bowl, the World Series, The World Cup, any mayor sports event when the season nears the end. Two teams come together to fight the ultimate battle on their field, for the victory and the trophies and recognition, along with their big fat bonuses if they win. No matter what the sport is, players on those teams prepare themselves for that day. They buffet their bodies, sharpening their minds, and focusing on the task of winning. They meticulously practice repeatedly to gain speed, accuracy, and strength. Everything they do is focused on the goal to win.

Shouldn't we as Christians have an even greater focus by preparing ourselves daily for the battle of life? For there is a race we are called to run (see Hebrews 12:1-2). And finally, in most all competitive sports, there is some type of equipment to wear. It's there to protect. As Christians, we too have equipment we're to wear.

We're commanded to put on the armor of God. That's the *equipment* we use to win. In Ephesians 6 we read, "Stand firm then, with the **belt of truth** buckled around your waist, with the **breastplate of righteousness** in place, and with your **feet fitted** with the readiness that comes from the gospel of peace. In addition to all this, take up the **shield of faith**, with which you can extinguish all the flaming arrows of the evil one. Take the **helmet of salvation** and the **sword of the Spirit,** which is the word of God. **And pray in the Spirit** on all occasions with all kinds of prayers and requests. With this in mind, be alert and always keep on praying for all the Lord's people" (emphasis mine).

Yet again I am reminded of how many Christians, myself included, have stayed in the holy huddles, brushing elbows with my fellow Christians, never fully engaging in the game, the battle, the one that

Remember, Christ has already given us victory (see 1 Corinthians 15:57)! We are more than conquerors (see Romans 8:37)! We have overcome the evil one by the blood of the Lamb (see Revelation 12:11)!

The Lens You Look Through

For since the creation of the world
His invisible *attributes* **are clearly seen**
Romans 1:20a (Emphasis mine)

I wear glasses. I wear them, so I can read and see clearly. If I take them off, I can still see, but things become fuzzy, especially words. For those of you that wear glasses, I'm sure you can relate to this. The title is, *The Lens You Look Through,* I would add, *it determines your destiny.*

As you know, there are all sorts of lenses. There are reading glasses, there are sunglasses, there are contact lenses, there are binoculars, there are camera lenses, there are telescopes, and probably others I've not mentioned.

These lenses help sharpen the focus, or to make things clear. If you didn't have these lenses, words, distance, focus with a camera, and other objects would be impossible to see with the naked eye, your vision would be blurry, and you might not even be able to see certain things at all.

The Bible says in Proverbs 29:18, "Where *there is* no vision, the people are unrestrained, but happy *is* he who keeps the law."

In other words, where people do not see the Bible as the Word of God, they cannot understand it, they can't see it clearly. They have no morals, no beliefs, they live for pleasure, and do what they want. But a person who understands God's word, and has a relationship with Him, is more than happy to keep His word.

How you look at life and how you look at God's word, through *spiritual vision* determines where you will spend an eternity.

A common argument takes place in many walks of life at this point. But since we can't openly debate this in person, let me propose something to you, if you're one that doubts the validity of the Bible, or perhaps the very existence of God, by asking you a couple of questions.

First, do you know absolutely everything about everything, and there is nothing you do not know? Of course, the answer from a reasonable person would be, as I'm sure you are, that you'd have to admit that you don't know everything. Right?

So, here's the second question. Since you logically admit that you don't know everything, is it possible for God to exist outside of the knowledge that you have? Once again, a reasonable person would also have to conclude that. And if God could be there, could He not have inspired the authors of the Scriptures to write exactly what He wanted us to know?

You see, since we're talking about *seeing,* we need to grasp the truth that you may not be able to adequately see God or His word as you should, because you've been wearing the wrong *lenses,* you have not been looking for God, or looking at His word correctly.

The Bible says in Romans 1 starting at verse 16; "For I am not ashamed of the gospel of Christ, for it is the **power** of God to **salvation** for everyone **who believes,** for the Jew first and also for the Greek. [17] For in it the righteousness of God is revealed from faith to faith; as it is written, 'The just shall live by faith'" (emphasis mine). In those 2 verses I see God's power, His plan (salvation), and his provision (believe, eternal life).

But God warns those who do not see clearly in verses 18-25:

"For the wrath of God is revealed from heaven against all ungodliness and unrighteousness of men, who suppress [hold down] the truth in unrighteousness, [19] because what may be known of God is manifest [made known] in them, for God has shown *it* to them. [20] For since the creation of the world His invisible *attributes* **are clearly seen,** being understood by the things that are made, *even* His eternal power and Godhead, so that they are without excuse, [21] because, although they knew God, they did not glorify *Him* as God, nor were thankful, but became futile in their thoughts, and their foolish hearts were darkened. **22** Professing to be wise, they became fools, **23** and changed the glory of the incorruptible God into an image made like corruptible man—and birds and four-footed animals and creeping things. **24** Therefore God also gave them up to uncleanness, in the **lusts of their hearts** [cf. 1 John 2:16], to dishonor their bodies among themselves, **25** who exchanged the truth of God for the lie and worshiped and served the creature rather than the Creator, who is blessed forever. Amen" (Romans 1:18-25, emphasis and comments in brackets are mine).

There was a day that I did not see things as I do now. There was a day that I did not really believe that Jesus loved me, and that He died to offer forgiveness for my sin. There was a day that I did not see the Bible clearly, not because of not having glasses, but because of the spiritual vision I didn't have.

Perhaps today you think you are okay, you are doing fine on your own, you don't need any God to help you see clearly and understand the Bible.

May I remind you of what we just read in Romans, it says, "Professing to be wise, they became fools." One other major roadblock in someone coming to understand that they need Jesus, that they need to confess their sins, ask for forgiveness, and surrender their hearts to him, is pride.

However, if while reading this today, you have felt a powerful desire in your heart to change the way you see things, what that is, is the power of God through the Holy Spirit.

Please do not harden your hearts toward the Holy Spirit at work in you. Respond to it by surrendering your heart and your life completely to Him now. I invite you to come to Jesus (see Appendix — Coming to Christ).

The Power of One

Then Moses said to the Lord, "O my Lord, I *am* not eloquent, neither before nor since You have spoken to Your servant; but I *am* slow of speech and slow of tongue." So, the Lord said to him, "Who has made man's mouth? Or who makes the mute, the deaf, the seeing, or the blind? *Have* not I, the Lord?"
Exodus 4:10-11

I'm going to start with a complaint, so fasten your seatbelts. I'll also throw it out as a question to see if anyone else has been in the same boat as me. Have you ever had an obstacle (tree, sign, car, building, bush, etc.) block your view while driving or pulling out from somewhere? Before I go any further, I have a confession.

Years ago, when I used to work as a manager where I had to test drive cars, and go on the same route each time, I had an obstacle blocking my view when approaching a busy street and I had to inch my way out to *try* and see if any cars were coming. It was an oil change facility that would put a sign advertising their special of the day, on the sidewalk, blocking my view, and I'm sure everyone else's when trying to pull out.

Ready for the confession? I made a *fake call* to that business acting like I was with the city sign ordinance department and told them they were in violation of some law I made up. My guess is you're either laughing and picking yourself up from the floor or shaking your head in disgust that I'd do something like that. Well, it worked. I know, I know, it was wrong, please forgive me.

I made up for it (sort of) 20+ years later and went about a similar complaint according to the rules. It's a bush. Right in the way, well... you guessed it, in the path of oncoming cars, to be able to see clearly pulling out onto a street, not far from where I live. You must inch out to be able to see cars in the righthand lane. Close enough to where they might have to dodge your front bumper when the go by.

So, I found the City website, found the right department, found the right issue that needed to be addressed, and after filling out my contact information, hit the online send button, never really expecting and answer, let alone results. Are you ready for this? In less than 2 weeks from when I submitted my complaint, *they cut the bush down!* I even called my wife and told her. *"Sweetheart, have you ever heard of the expression, "the power of one"?*

Maybe I wasn't the only one to file a complaint about that bush, but for as long as it had been there, I really must wonder. So, you see, I was just one person and made a difference. Maybe, just maybe I saved a future accident from happening? Well, you never know!

There're other types of stories about *the power of one,* and those are the ones that get our attention. They are the stories about the underdogs, right? You know, that one kid that everyone picks on? Maybe he'll end up being mentored by a guy that owns a Karate studio and before you know it, he'll be able to defend himself from the bullies. Or, that timid, sort of awkward gal at the office, the one who wears the thick rimmed glasses, the one that can never get a date? Someone will take her on as a *project* at a beauty salon and before you know it, she's got every guy around trying to take her out.

We've always been attracted to shows and movies like that, and after all, who would ever root for the bully anyway? He's a jerk (sorry, but it's true) on the outside and has some serious insecurities too. But hey, even some of those guys turn out by the end of the scripts to have a change of heart.

Whether it's in a movie, or even in sports, we always like an underdog to win. Did you know that God's word is full of underdogs too? If you've ever heard of the *Heroes of Faith* in Hebrews chapter 11, they were all underdogs.

Which brings me back to the verse at the beginning of this chapter. Look at his life throughout Scripture and see if you think he wasn't and underdog. In fact, today we might say he was a looser from the beginning. A basket case in the Nile. A Hebrew in and Egyptian home school. A guy who took matters into his own hands, including the life of another man. And a runaway and a vagabond. Sounds like a guy primed and ready to be used by God, right? Not quite. He had to go to the school of hard knocks for the next 40 years before God could use him. And use him, did He ever!

Moses, *The Power of One* ONLY because God used him, despite his lack of communication skills, leadership ability, and an entire Nation of people that wanted to trade him in every time the journey to the Promised Land was doubtful (which was often).

What about you? Can you make a difference? You're *only* one person, who's going to listen to you, right? History is full of people that were not willing to take no for an answer. Some were rejected countless times, but they had a passion for what they believed in, and many of them God used to change millions of lives.

Billy Graham. Abe Lincoln. Sir Isaac Newton. Noah. Benjamin Franklin. Joseph. Christopher Columbus. Rahab. Albert Einstein. Paul. Henry Ford. King David. Martin Luther King Jr. Samuel. William Tyndale. Harland Sanders.

I could fill up pages of people who changed history, so I'll end my brief list with that. My point should be clear, people can make a difference. One voice, one crying in the wilderness (like John the Baptist).

I'll close with the mention of *One* more, *one* that would change the course of humanity for eternity, the *One* that said, "I am the way, the truth, and the life. No one comes to the Father except through Me" (John 14:6). Now that's The Power of One!

The Way of Self—Unforgiveness

Then Peter came to Jesus and asked, "Lord, how many times shall I forgive my brother or sister who sins against me? Up to seven times?" Jesus answered, "I tell you, not seven times, but seventy-seven times."
Matthew 18:21-22 (NIV)

The simplest explanation I have ever heard about unforgiveness is this: *"Holding onto anger (or unforgiveness) is like drinking poison and expecting the other person to die from it."* It has been my experience that many people who are unforgiving carry that with them into other areas of life. It will affect their attitude, rob them of their joy, make them bitter, and possibly even sick physically. Most often I have found that the very ones they are not willing to forgive have long since forgot what something was all about and moved on in life. All the while the bitter (unforgiving) person gets worse and worse. Unforgiveness can be like a cancer that spreads and if left untreated will eventually take the life out of you; emotionally, relationally, physically.

The writer of Hebrews in chapter 12:14-15 clearly explains what can fester when unforgiveness exists. "Pursue peace with all *people*, and holiness, without which no one will see the Lord: looking carefully lest anyone fall short of the grace of God; lest any root of bitterness springing up cause trouble, and by this many become defiled;"

Looking back at my life I can see periods where I had an unforgiving heart and I know how it affected me and even my relationship with God. I felt like a hypocrite, not forgiving people I feel did something to me to hurt me.

I remember a time in my life where I had bitterness toward a couple for what they had done. Even when I tried to confront them, they excused their actions away and gave reason for it and even blurted out a 'sorry' but the way it was said was not from their heart. I took this to the Lord knowing it could eat me up from the inside out if not dealt with. Because God is faithful and hears our prayers and knows our hearts, He answered me and almost not realizing it myself I found that unforgiveness was removed from my heart and I now love this brother and sister as I did before the offense. I've found myself not even remembering it at all, praise God.

So, what happens to those who do not forgive others the way God has forgiven them? Back to the verse at the beginning of this chapter. A parable Jesus gave about forgiveness after Peter asked the question in Matthew 18:21. The servant, who represents us, owed his master, representing God, a huge debt. So, large in fact, that he could never repay it—never. Suddenly he is forgiven. Then, however, he completely forgets what happened and finds a fellow servant that owed him next to nothing and demanded very harshly that he pay up. At any time, we find ourselves even coming close to having an unforgiving attitude, we should quickly remind ourselves of the huge debt we owed God, the one we could never pay him for (our sin) and freely offer to forgive anyone, anything they have done to hurt us—which most of the time is very small in the first place.

Is there any unforgiveness in your heart? Oh, how I pray if there is any unforgiveness in my heart that God reveals it to me, takes me to the woodshed, and corrects me as only He can. By His word I want to look continually at my heart and see if there's anything in me that has not forgiven someone. God knows my heart, but I know my heart as well. Based on His word I know how I can be too. In Jeremiah 17:9 we read, "The heart *is* deceitful above all *things*, and desperately wicked; who can know it?"

Because of that, I must continually examine my heart and ask God to reveal any sin in my life toward others. Take time to examine your heart. There are some great passages to read and mediate on regarding this. Psalm 26:2, "Test me, LORD, and try me, examine my heart and my mind" (NIV). Psalm 139:23, "Search me, God, and know my heart; test me and know my anxious thoughts" (NLT). Lamentations 3:40, "Let us search out and examine our ways, and turn back to the LORD."

Here's another question for you. How do we ultimately let go of unforgiveness when we do not have the ability to forget or wipe out the memory as God does? ONLY by prayer and confession of our sin, which is what unforgiveness is, can we ever forgive AND forget about an offense against us. We must look at others in the same way God looks at us. We must take the Living Word of God and allow it to transform our lives and especially our hearts.

I love the words in Colossians 3:12-13; "Putting on" as in clothing ourselves with the word and letting it surround us and envelope us: "Therefore, as *the* elect of God, holy and beloved, put on tender mercies, kindness, humility, meekness, longsuffering; bearing with one another, and forgiving one another, if anyone has a complaint against another, even as Christ forgave you, so you also *must do*."

James 5:16 is a perfect example of how to go about healing our minds through forgiving others. "Therefore confess your sins to each other and pray for each other so that you may be healed. The prayer of a righteous person is powerful and effective" (NIV). Healing—isn't that what God wants from our hearts? Isn't that the type of attitude He wants us to have towards a brother and sister? So, if we are offended, or if we offend, or let's call it what it really is: *sin*. Then we should go to our brother, confess our sin [unforgiveness] and pray with each other, and through the power of the cross and the resurrection of Jesus Christ will be healed from that unforgiving heart.

When Jesus calls us to serve Him, we should be excited and eager to do our best. But quite often we find out that things would go a whole lot smoother in life if our circumstances were better, if finances weren't so tight, if that person at church with different ideas wouldn't be in leadership, if we wouldn't have to work with that other person with their overbearing personality. As time goes by, our initial excitement wears off, and the irritations, disappointments and conflicts with others seem to get stronger. Finally, we get to the point where we can't take much more, and one of two things happens; we start pushing for our rights or we walk away hurt and bitter.

Why do you think it is that sometimes we can't survive in serving the Lord, even though we started with such willing and sincere hearts? Could it be that we forgot that we're in a battle that wages war not against flesh and blood? We end up fighting those around us instead of the real enemy. Did we prepare ourselves properly for the spiritual battle as Paul describes in Ephesians? If our answer is yes, what else are we missing?

Our answer is found in the word. 1 Peter 4:1a says: "Therefore, since Christ suffered for us in the flesh, arm yourselves also with the same mind." Have we armed ourselves with a willingness to suffer—to the same extent that Christ suffered while He lived here on the earth? The idea of suffering does not fit our 21st-century concept of following and serving Jesus. But the Bible teaches that suffering for Him is a privilege: "For to you it has been granted on behalf of Christ, not only to believe in Him, but also to suffer for His sake" (Philippians 1:29).

You may not suffer as those during Jesus' lifetime, or the persecution that takes place in third-world countries, but you may be suffering from what I've been talking about here – unforgiveness. And maybe, just maybe as I've mentioned, it's eating away at you like cancer. I hope and pray the Scripture and thoughts I've shared with you, will give you a new perspective on giving up that unforgiving heart.

"Father, many times in life we fail and fall short of what You would want us to be. For You have called us to be conquerors, and by dwelling on past hurts in our lives can only create a road-block in future relationships, not to mention my relationship with You. Lord, first, forgive my unforgiving heart. Take me back to the foot of the cross, where I first experienced Your overwhelming forgiveness. Cleanse me, purify me, give me a tender and forgiving heart, in Jesus Name, Amen."

The Way of Jesus—Forgiveness

But He was wounded for our transgressions, *He was* bruised for
our iniquities; The chastisement for our peace *was* upon Him,
and by His stripes we are healed.
Isaiah 53:5

In a previous chapter, I mentioned watching the movie, *The
Passion of the Christ*. I went with a group of friends to a theatre one night
shortly after it came out. Aside from the time that both my parents
passed away, I have never wept so hard in my entire life. Inside I wept. I
didn't cry as much externally as I did internally. I hurt for the realization
of what the verse above clearly explains, *He was wounded... He was
bruised... He had (our) stripes on His back.*

That's our Jesus. The sinless, spotless Lamb of God. The One who
lived to die, so that He can conquer death once and for all. The death we
deserved. Why? So that we may have everlasting life with Him. He offers
forgiveness. Genuine forgiveness. *The slate is clean, the records are
expunged, the penalty is paid, kind of forgiveness.*

Now before I lose you with where we're going, let's jump right in
as if we have just finished mowing the lawn on a hot, muggy day in 90-
degree weather and the swimming pool is calling our name begging for
us to come and jump in to the cool, refreshing, water (personal
experience).

The title of this chapter is, *The Way of Jesus—Forgiveness*. The
obvious question to ask then is, what is *the way of Jesus*? Can we really
be like Him? Is it possible to be, as the Scripture refers to, being *Christ
like*? Having the *mind-set* of Jesus? (see Philippians 2:1-5).

Remember now, I just tied together two important things about
Jesus. In case you missed it, read all the above again. Did you see it that
time? That's right, the simple equation is this; *to be like Jesus is to*

forgive—the slate is clean, the records are expunged, that kind of forgiveness.

Lewis B. Smedes wrote, "When you release the wrongdoer from the wrong, you cut a malignant tumor out of your inner life. You set a prisoner free, but you discover that the real prisoner was yourself."[27]

Forgiveness goes against our human nature, but to forgive is the genuine, willful act of letting go of a hurt, a wrong against you, be it real or imagined. Forgiveness is forgetting what happened and looking at a person as if the offense never took place. It prevents us from dwelling on past troubles. The best way to forgive someone is to pray for them and ask God to give you new eyes and a new heart toward them to see them and love them like He sees you and loves you.

Colossians 3:12-13 Paul gives specific instructions on what do; "Therefore, as *the* elect of God, holy and beloved, put on tender mercies, kindness, humility, meekness, long-suffering; bearing with one another, and forgiving one another, if anyone has a complaint against another; even as Christ forgave you, so you also *must do*."

He also writes In Ephesians 4:31-32; "Let all bitterness, wrath, anger, clamor, and evil speaking be put away from you, with all malice. And be kind to one another, tenderhearted, forgiving one another, even as God in Christ forgave you."

In the Lord's Prayer recorded in Matthew, chapter 6 and verse 12, Jesus says we are to pray, "And forgive us our debts, as we forgive our debtors."

May I remind you what we covered in the previous chapter about the parable in Matthew 18? Peter I'm sure, thinking he sounded somewhat self-righteous in even proposing this question, (since at that time, according to Jewish law, forgiving up to three times was all that was

---

[27] Lewis B. Smedes, *Forgive and Forget,* thoughtco.com/enlightening-forgiveness-quotes-701566 (accessed, December 12, 2018).

expected) said; "Lord, how often shall my brother sin against me, and I forgive him? Up to seven times?" (Matthew 18:21).

Jesus took Peter's "seven times," multiplied it "seventy times seven" (not meaning we are to keep count of the four hundred ninety times and then no more) and gave another parable about a forgiving master and a wicked, unforgiving slave, in which He concluded with his point: "So My Heavenly Father also will do to you [not forgive] if each of you, from his heart, does not forgive his brother his trespasses" (Matthew 18:35; comment in brackets mine). This ties together the forgiveness we are to have with one another based on the forgiveness we have from God. Something we should never forget.

So, the forgiveness that we receive from God when we ask of Him should not be confused with the forgiveness we receive through repentance at salvation. First off, forgiveness is freely offered to anyone who has already come to the cross and repented of their sins and received salvation—because it is restoring a relationship between a man and his God. Although positionally we are perfect in Christ, we are still living in the flesh and do have a sin nature, and we do sin. Therefore, when we do sin we need to confess it, ask for forgiveness, that which He has already freely given us, and our relationship is then restored.

For example, in Psalm 32 when David wrote about his sin with Bathsheba, he was clearly a man who had already walked with God; we know that from his youth before he was king and before his sin with her. David wrote this after his sin and after coming back to God and asking Him for forgiveness. "I acknowledged my sin to You, and my iniquity I have not hidden. I said, 'I will confess my transgressions to the Lord;' And You forgave the iniquity of my sin" (Psalm 32:5).

In Romans 8:1, Paul writes, "*There is* therefore now no condemnation [because we've been forgiven] to those who are in Christ Jesus, who do not walk according to the flesh, but according to the Spirit" (comment in brackets mine).

Matthew 26:27-28 says, "Then He took the cup, and gave thanks, and gave *it* to them, saying, 'Drink from it, all of you. For this is My blood of the new covenant, which is shed for many for the remission [forgiveness] of sins'" (comment mine).

And Peter said in Acts 10:43, "To Him all the prophets witness that, through His name, whoever believes in Him will receive remission of sins."

And finally, in Colossians 1:13-14 we have a clear picture of who we are in Christ; "He has delivered us from the power of darkness and conveyed *us* into the kingdom of the Son of His love, in whom we have redemption through His blood, the forgiveness of sins."

Only you can answer this question, *"has God forgiven you?"* For me personally, the truth lies in my salvation (repentance, turning from evil and turning to God—receiving His grace, nothing I did) because God promised to forgive me, and God is the original PROMISE KEEPER! In 1 John 1:9 we read, "If we confess our sins, he is faithful and just to forgive us *our* sins, and to cleanse us from **all** unrighteousness" (emphasis mine). The *only* sin God will never forgive is the one we fail to bring to Him.

So, if God forgives us, does He keep a record of our sins for the next time we sin? In Psalm 103:12 the Bible says; "As far as the east is from the west, so far has He removed our transgressions from us." God chooses not to remember our sin after we are forgiven. In Isaiah 43:25 God says "I, *even* I, *am* He who blots out your transgressions for My own sake; and I will not remember your sins." He doesn't do it for us, although we are the beneficiaries of His forgiveness, He says He did it for HIS sake. Just like the children of Israel that sinned time and time again—God said He saved them for HIS Name sake! He also reckons us (settling the account of sin against us and wiping the slate clean) dead to sin and the penalty of it through His son's death on the cross; He looks at us through the lens of that act on Calvary. This choosing that God does, not to remember our sin anymore, is beyond our comprehension.

The very foundation of forgiveness is the shed Blood of Jesus Christ which paid the price for our sins, and which made it possible for God to justly forgive us. It is critical to see that God's forgiveness was never based on anything we did or currently do. God sent Jesus to die for our sin, and offer us forgiveness, completely independent of anything about us. In fact, God says that "the Lamb [Jesus Christ] was slain before the foundation of the world" in Revelation 13:8 (bracketed words mine). God's forgiveness was previously applied as finished before the foundation of the world, *millennia* before any of us were born! Romans 5:8 says, "But God demonstrates His own love toward us, in that while we were still sinners, Christ died for us." I don't know about you, but my finite mind has problems processing that one.

I experienced the forgiveness of my Heavenly Father through the shed blood of His son, Jesus Christ, but I have experienced human forgiveness too. The type of human forgiveness that has literally enlightened me to a new awareness of the forgiveness of my Savior.

A few years ago, I was visiting a friend that was being cared for at a hospice facility. Although our friendship had been broken for years after his divorce, healing and forgiveness took place after we reconnected. During those absent years, he was suffering spiritually and emotionally, however, by the grace of God, and the forgiveness of God, he came back full circle. Even in his weakness he kept smiling, praising God, and was a living testimony in my eyes of the God we both love with all our hearts. As I was showing him some pictures that night from several years ago, and one of my sweet wife, I shared with him what took place in my life not long ago.

During a revival summit at our church, being under the conviction of the word of God and the Spirit of God, I confessed to my wife of 34 years, of my moral failures from many years ago, before I surrendered my life to Jesus. She had every right to divorce me, and I thought she would, or at least if she were to put up with me she would hate me or punish me for it and never let me forget it. But on the contrary, after some time to heal and process it (most certainly praying much over it) she forgave me completely.

We reconciled completely and ever since then I have fallen in love with her all over again and have grown to appreciate her as the woman God gave me. Her act of forgiving me brought me to a new appreciation of the forgiveness God so freely gave me, and the forgiveness I too need to freely offer to others.

After reading this chapter and the one prior on unforgiveness, I pray that the Holy Spirit has been at work in your life, pricking your heart, recalling relationships that need healing and forgiving. So, I'm offering you the opportunity right now, wherever you are reading this, to stop, bow your head, and pour out your heart to the Lord. Ask Him to give you a new heart, ready, willing, and only able according to His word, to forgive.

Walking Dead

And you *He made alive*, who were **dead** in trespasses and sins, in which you once **walked** according to the course of this world, according to the prince of the power of the air, the spirit who now works in the sons of disobedience, among whom also we all once conducted ourselves in the lusts of our flesh, fulfilling the desires of the flesh and of the mind, and were by nature children of wrath, just as the others.
Ephesians 2:1-3 (Emphasis mine)

Be honest, after reading that title what was the first thing that came to your mind? A tv show by that title, right? After all, where else have you heard those two words put together (unless it describes your co-workers on a Monday morning). The only familiarity I have with that show, is having heard about it, or saw a commercial about. Personally, walking dead people with morbid faces is the last thing I want to subject my mind to.

On a more serious note, separate the thought of that show from your mind and allow me to help you understand what exactly I meant by the title.

As you've already read in this book, I believe I was saved sometime around the age of 14 years old. However, that does not mean that everything was uphill or moving forward in my walk and growth as a Christian. I had many fall backs, many wanderings, many doubts personally, acting like a lost man at times. How on earth could I be a Christian and act like that?

I have heard it said before, I believe it was from the late Dr. Adrian Rogers, that *the most miserable man on earth is not a lost man, but a saved man that is not walking in fellowship with God.* That was me at times. I felt as if I was *Walking Dead.*

One such period of my life was not long after my wife and I were married, and we had one child. Even now as I think about what to share with you, I struggle with those memories. Some of the things that took place, I can picture vividly in my mind, and I see a man that I am ashamed to admit was me.

It wasn't the first time my life exhibited a Dr. Jekyll and Mr. Hyde lifestyle. It may not be the last (see Jeremiah 17:9-10), but I hope and pray by the grace of God that it will never repeat itself or happen again. To some people I was one person, to others I was totally different. You do that when you're a self-seeking, selfish, prideful sinner as I was. Yes, although I believe I was saved, it didn't mean I was perfect and sinless.

I see no reason to give any more details other than to say that alcohol and women were a consuming sinful lifestyle of mine. It nearly cost me my family at the time. I can only thank God for reminding me of His forgiveness, by using my brother's wedding to turn my life back on track toward Him.

I have a question for you before we go further. What about you? What is your life like? Is the person everyone sees on the outside the same person that is on the inside (your heart and mind)? This is where you're going to take a personal inventory. "Examine yourselves, whether ye be in the faith; **prove** your own selves. Know ye not your own selves, how that Jesus Christ is in you, except ye be reprobates?" (2 Corinthians 13:5; KJV).

The word *prove* in that verse means a proof other people will see on the outside, because of what's taking place on the inside. That word *prove* also means to test, scrutinize, to see whether a thing is genuine or not, such as the way metal is tested. You see the difference? A straightforward way to put it is, *"What's down in the well, comes up in the bucket."*

Too often when the heart of a person is not totally surrendered to Jesus Christ as Lord and Savior (and it *can* even happen then), theirs is a progression of falling away from the Lord that takes place. It's the *frog in the kettle* scenario.

Casting Crowns[28] has a song that illustrates what can happen to a person whose heart is not committed to the Lord. The song is called, *Slow Fade.* I'd like you to search the Internet for the lyrics and read them. I encourage you to do that right now, before you finish this chapter. It simply begins with, "Be careful little eyes what you see, It's the second glance that ties your hands as darkness pulls the strings... It's a slow fade."

I have some unfortunate news for you before I go any further. Whatever plagued you before you came to Christ, in other words, your weaknesses, your temptations, your sins, those are the things Satan will use against you in his attempt to bring you back down. If you are not being tempted, if everything in life is just going great, and you never have thoughts toward those earlier sins, I mean, you are just the perfect little example of a Christian, then you'd better take inventory of your relationship with Jesus Christ. Because, you are not doing anything to hinder the work of the devil, so he's leaving you alone.

If, however, you are being bombarded with the attacks of the enemy, then you must be doing something for Jesus. But even in those valleys of the shadow of death (see Psalm 23) don't fear, put on the armor (see Ephesians 6:10-17).

There's one more thing I want to add and then I'll conclude. What are we, those that believe we have surrendered our lives to the Lord, to do daily? I've said it before; well, Paul originated it in 1 Peter 3:15 ("always *be* ready to *give* a defense to everyone who asks you a reason for the hope that is in you"), we are also called to be ambassadors for the sake of the kingdom (see 2 Corinthians 5:20). Which all means, those around us, the lost souls that look like the *walking dead,* they really are. They have no hope without Jesus Christ.

Share the hope, share your testimony, pray, pray, and then pray more that God will draw others to Himself (see John 12:32). It is His will

---

[28] Christian band (website at: castingcrowns.com). For more info, see: *Wikipedia, The Free Encyclopedia*, s.v. "Casting Crowns," (accessed, December 12, 2018), https://en.wikipedia.org/wiki/Casting_Crowns

that none are lost. Don't let the arguments interfere with you sharing the gospel with others, it is God at work in us that will take His servants, and direct them to the lost and dying world, and use His word, to illuminate the hearts of others. It should be our hearts desire to see the *walking dead,* ALIVE!

You Go Where You Look

But Jesus said to him, "No one, having put his hand to the plow, and
looking back, is fit for the kingdom of God."
Luke 9:62

Never in my life as the title of this article states, has this truth
been more prevalent. In a practical sense, since I ride a motorcycle, what
it means to me could even be fatal if you look away from where you
should be going. If you ride too, then you know the truth of that
statement. If you're in doubt as to the truth of this statement, then try it
sometime, but be careful or you'll wind up crashing and burning. It
doesn't take much either; a casual look to the right or left and you can
shift from one lane to another, into another biker, off the road or even
into oncoming traffic. You go where you look!

This is not only true when riding a motorcycle, but I would say it's
even more so in your spiritual journey; whatever that may look like to
you, but I mean it through the Christian life especially.

One of my most favorite passages in the Bible and what I call my
life verse, is found in Hebrews 12:1-2. "Therefore we also, since we are
surrounded by so great a cloud of witnesses [see chapter 11] let us lay
aside every weight, and the sin which so easily ensnares *us*, and let us run
with endurance the race that is set before us, **looking unto Jesus**,
[another translation has: **fixing our eyes on Jesus**] the author and finisher
of *our* faith, who for the joy that was set before Him endured the cross,
despising the shame, and has sat down at the right hand of the throne of
God" (emphasis and comments in brackets are mine).

If you want to know the best way to start backsliding or if you
want your heart to start crowing cold to the things the Lord wants you to
do, just make it a habit of taking your eyes off Jesus. I promise you on the
authority of the word of God that you will start a "slow fade" of a life

filled with bitterness, hate towards others and before you know it you will "crash and burn" as an individual.

But seriously, who would ever get up one morning and say, "I think today I'll begin to ruin my life, throw away all that I have, turn my back on all those I love, and mess up my life so bad, that I end up walking away from God?"

Yet, it happens to the most well-meaning individuals. Slowly, over time, taking looks in the wrong direction, a heart grows cold towards the Lord. Over and over a person may look in the mirror and say to the one looking back, "who are you and what have you become?"

I believe that there is a slow process in which takes place over time, as a believer who once walked closely with the Lord, turns their back by looking away from where they should. It happens riding a motorcycle, it happens in yours and my life if we are not careful to "fix our eyes on Jesus."

Here are 10 steps to what some call backsliding, or the result of looking where you shouldn't have, then you go in that direction. If you want to make sure you are keeping your eyes fixed on Jesus, then look at this list and make sure you're not living like this or I can promise you that you have already gone where you looked, away from Jesus. The dangers of taking the course below can not only destroy your life, all those around you, but have an eternal impact on your soul.

1. You begin to spend more time thinking about worldly things, other than God's word; you become pre-occupied in your thought life with fun things to do, and pleasure becomes a priority.
2. You begin to neglect your once private spiritual exercises, perhaps out of guilt, or what is called your daily quiet-time, one-on-one with the Lord.
3. Sometimes, just after the first two steps, friends notice something wrong in your life, and you start to turn away from the fellowship you once had with them.
4. Instead of facing your friends and turn back toward Christ and turning your eyes on Him again, seeking forgiveness, you drop out

of those once trusted Christian circles and relationships, finding it better for you not to face them any longer.

5. You become increasingly critical of the actions and words of others, those who you once considered genuine friends, family members, those who gently attempt at talking with you in love and deep concern.

6. You start hanging around with more unbelievers and those whose lifestyles at one point you thought would have a negative impact on you; now those same people start to impact you after all.

7. You begin not only to act like those mentioned above, but now you sound like them as well. Cursing becomes the norm, and on occasion, the use of your once loved Lords name in vain and ugly ways.

8. What used to make you feel guilty, that which was practiced behind closed doors in fear of others finding you out, is now openly participated in almost daily, those sins that you don't even blush after anymore.

9. Your heart now grows hard, to the point that most all actions are for selfish gain, you are always right, and nothing anyone says to you in love, trying to guide you back, is accepted; pleasure, self-seeking, cold-heartedness towards Christianity prevails.

10. You are now at a point of being considered an unbeliever. Treated like one. Maybe you are one. This is toying with your eternal destination (see Appendix—Coming to Christ).

I have seen it personally happen, time and time again. The progression of sin: I have personally experienced it before. We are all like the old hymn says, *"Prone to wander, Lord I feel it, Prone to leave the God I love."*

175

Zoey

So Samuel said: "Has the LORD as great delight in burnt
offerings and sacrifices, as in obeying the voice of the LORD?
Behold, to obey is better than sacrifice"
1 Samuel 15:22

Please don't be offended by what you're about to read, just bear
with me and you'll see how I tie this together. I'd like to illustrate my
relationship with my dog, Zoey, in comparison with my relationship with
God. Just hang on, extend me a little grace, okay?

Zoey is the name I picked out for our puppy almost 3 years ago.
There's no doubt about who's her daddy either. Yes, that's me. She is
what the vet describes as a Lab-mix. Rescued from the middle of a rural
road during an ice storm along with her brother. Rescue. Think about that
word for a second.

We use that word in many ways. A person overboard or lost at sea
gets rescued, hopefully. A person in a burning building is rescued by a
fireman. A person that doesn't know God, is what we call *lost*. What do
they need? Well, besides God, they need to be rescued, they need to be
saved.

I think you see my point. Which has a little to do with what I'm
about to share. Sort of. You'll see.

Zoey is what I would call, well...unique. I guess you could say she
has her own story too, just like we all do. Not the rescue story, I mean the
story she's written in our lives for the past 3 years. I won't tell you all the
details, besides, I know some of you aren't even animal lovers to begin
with. But don't worry, those of us that are love you anyway.

Being the responsible pet owners that we are, of course we
enrolled Zoey in obedience school. After all, Oliver, our Puggle went, so
why shouldn't Zoey, right? Now Baylee, our outside kitten (okay, she's 9

years old but she's still my kitty) she was just so smart when we got her, she didn't need school. But then again, have you ever seen someone out walking their cat?

So, just as Zoey had to learn obedience in certain areas, like sit, leave it, okay, come, walk, place, and on they go, she also needed to learn to obey me when I call her name. She got a D- in that subject. Which leads me to a story about her. Hang on, I promise this is going somewhere.

Since we brought Zoey home, she became my responsibility to potty-train (oh boy) and in the early days, that meant getting up about every 2 hours. She's much, much better now and has slept through the night for quite a while now. But, she has this morning routine that has tried my patience.

Her morning routine is, right after I get up, I let her out in the backyard. Our cat, Baylee, sometimes stays in the garage overnight if it's cold outside. They greet each other when I open the door, and then Zoey goes right to the backyard to do her thing. But I discovered some time ago, that Zoey likes to 'play' with Baylee when she's ready to get out of the garage after being in there all night, to hop our fence to go do her thing. If Bayless isn't in the garage overnight, she jumps over the fence to come *into* the garage, creating the same scenario.

It took me a while after this game started to find Zoey's little hiding place. It's under the kid's rock-wall and slide. She's jet black, and it's very dark when I get up, so I can't exactly see her well. The reason she hides there is she's waiting to chase Baylee as she exits the garage towards the fence line or come over the fence and go to the garage.

What makes matters worse after the chase, if it has rained and it's muddy back there, I have 4 very messy paws to clean-up before she comes back into the house. You see, I have a routine too. This interrupts my morning routine. She misbehaves by waiting out there for Baylee after I've called her.

Even worse, after the chase, and after I've called her to come back inside, she still finds it necessary to roam the yard and sniff every square inch of it before she's satisfied to come in. I can be a little irritable at 4:30 in the morning truth-be-told.

She hears me calling her. She knows I care about her. She knows it's warmer inside when it's cold outside, it's safe from storms (which she hates), her daddy that rescued her provides everything she needs. But, she willingly disobeys.

I really hate to admit to it, but I have done the same thing to my daddy. Or should I say, my Abba. My Father. My Lord and Savior. What about you?

I'm even more to blame for my disobedience, because I'm not a dog, but a logical, thinking, human-being that knows right from wrong. Like when I was avoiding the call of the Lord, wading in the depth of sin in past times, knowing the Father was calling me, knowing there was peace, love, joy, grace, mercy, forgiveness, ALL waiting for me, yet waiting for the "Baylee's" in my life so I could chase them over the wall. Get my life all muddy. The Father, the only One that could *clean me.*

Zoey has a nature because she's a dog. That is what she was created to be. I have a nature as well. A dog's nature is to chase a cat. I think our disobedience to an all loving Father is our nature too—our sinful nature. The one we inherited from Adam. But the other nature, from the second Adam, Jesus Christ, that nature was changed. So, we are no longer slaves to sin (see Romans 6:16).

The verse at the beginning of this chapter, was written about King Saul, who had the choice to obey what Samuel instructed him to do (via God). But rather than obey what he was told, he took matters into his own hands. He was a *people pleaser* in the worst sense. He thought he'd gain favor from the people if the kept back some of what they were told to destroy. It cost him his crown and his throne, although not immediately, eventually. And even cost him his life.

Our sinful nature is bent toward selfishness and pride. However, as 1 Corinthians 10:13 says, even when we are tempted, we have a way of escape. Look it up.

Believe it or not Zoey taught me a lesson through her disobedience. Which incidentally, she has improved leaps and bounds with listening to me now. God can use the simplest things (even our pets) to teach us life lessons.

Isn't our God an Awesome God?

Appendix — Coming to Christ

Well, you're here, right where I was hoping you would come. Maybe you're even here before you finished reading all the devotions, that's perfectly okay. You're here, not because of anything I've written, but because the Holy Spirit has been prompting you, He's been knocking on the door of your heart. Whatever you do right now, please don't ignore that knock, open the door, invite Him in.

Inviting Him is so simple, even a child can understand it. If you've never completely surrendered your life to Jesus, you can do that right now. A surrender is lifting your hands up, whether physically, or from your heartfelt intents, empty hands showing you're holding on to nothing, to express your willingness to *give up* without any conditions. When one *surrenders* they're giving up all their rights, to the One they're giving themselves to.

Maybe you *think* you've had an *experience* in your past where you thought you became a Christian, maybe you walked down an aisle at a church, or prayed a certain prayer, or joined a church, and even went every Sunday; yet your life shows no fruit; wherever you find yourself right here, right now, you can end all the games, you can settle it once and for all, you can stop *trying* to *be good* enough. It doesn't matter where you're reading this, you can do something that you'll never, ever regret, I promise.

Pride will keep you from doing this, because pride says, "*I'm good, I don't need this right now, maybe later,*" or, "*yea, that sounds good, I'll add a little Jesus to my life to give me a good feeling, a ticket to heaven.*"

God doesn't want either of those things my friend, as I said, He wants total, complete, unconditional *surrender*.

The hardest part for those of you that think you're *okay* is admitting that you're a sinner. I hate to break the news to you, but you're hopelessly lost without Him. The Bible says, "all have sinned and come short of the glory of God" (Romans 3:23).

You can't be *good enough* to earn your way to heaven, "not by works of righteousness which we have done, but according to His mercy He saved us" (Titus 3:5). Believe by *faith,* trusting that God will save you. "For by grace you have been saved through faith, and that not of yourselves; it is the gift of God, not of works, lest anyone should boast" (Ephesians 2:8-9).

Read the verses below.

"But God demonstrates His own love toward us, in that while we were still sinners, Christ died for us." Romans 5:8

"But if we walk in the light as He is in the light, we have fellowship with one another, and the blood of Jesus Christ His Son cleanses us from all sin." 1 John 1:7

"So, they said, 'Believe on the Lord Jesus Christ, and you will be saved, you and your household.'" Acts 16:31

"Nor is there salvation in any other, for there is no other name under heaven given among men by which we must be saved." Acts 4:12

"Jesus said to him, 'I am the way, the truth, and the life. No one comes to the Father except through Me.'" John 14:6

"All that the Father gives Me will come to Me, and the one who comes to Me I will by no means cast out." John 6:37

"But as many as received Him, to them He gave the right to become children of God, to those who believe in His name." John 1:12

May I suggest you pray right now? Here's a suggestion if you'd like; "Dear God, I'm asking You right now to forgive my sins. I believe in you and that your word is true. I believe that Jesus died on the cross, to pay the penalty for my sin, so that I may have eternal life. I believe that You raised Him from the dead. I need a You Lord as my Savior now. I surrender my life to You God, right now, I give you my life and ask you to take full control from this moment on. I have a lot to learn God, help me from this moment on to trust You with my life and not rely on my feelings, but by faith, that you'll show me. I pray this in the name of Jesus, Amen

If you trusted in Jesus just now, if you know beyond a shadow of doubt that He saved you, would you do me a favor and email me and let me know so that I can pray for you? Even if the Lord used one or more of these devotionals to impact your life, I'd also love to hear from you.

fortydayjourney@hotmail.com

Made in the USA
Columbia, SC
20 January 2019